AF283925

Reflections on Lace

Reflections on Lace

Nenia Lovesey

A letter to my granddaughters.
For
Zaien, Elicia, Kate Marie,
Pippa Louise, Nena Maria,
Kate Louise, Olivia Fay,
and Emma Victoria.
Indeed
for any other little girl
with love from
Nana Lovesey.

Dryad Press Ltd London

ACKNOWLEDGMENT

I wish to acknowledge all the help I have had from Nina Devereux for her hard work redrawing many of the designs and helping to complete so much art work in so little time; Maureen Long for editing the script and for all the photocopying and a dozen or more jobs along the way, and my friends who have worked through so many of the designs in three short months, including Winnie Hunt, Joan Merrifield, Cathy Barley, Doreen Holmes, Nina Devereux, Vera Nichols, Babs Ingledew, Daphne Keen and not forgetting Pippa and Kate Marie.

My thanks to Ann Aldridge for allowing me to use so much from her collection, my daughter Claire Stares for the photography and to Mike Tilly for giving her his assistance and advice – and yet again to my husband Les. God bless him.

© Nenia Lovesey 1988
First published 1988

All rights reserved. No part of this publication
may be reproduced, in any form or by any means,
without permission from the Publisher

ISBN 0 8521 9750 0

Typeset by Keyspools Ltd, Golborne, Lancs
and printed in Great Britain by
The Bath Press Ltd
Bath
for the publishers
Dryad Press Ltd
8 Cavendish Square
London W1M 0AJ

British Library Cataloguing in Publication Data

Lovesey, Nenia
    Reflections on lace.
    1. Lace. Making. Manuals
    I. Title
    746.2′2

ISBN 0-85219-750-0

Contents

If you think the pattern is beyond your ken,
If your bobbins will not run or your stitches curl up,
Then, my darlings, read on.

If you think you are beaten, you are,
If you think you dare not, you don't,
If you like to win, but think you can't,
It's almost certain you won't.
If you think you'll lose, you are lost,
For out of this you would find
Success begins with a person's will,
It's all in the state of mind.

If you think you're outclassed, then you are,
You have to think 'high rise'.
You have to be sure of yourself before
You can ever win a prize.

Life's battles do not always go
To the strongest or fastest one,
But sooner or later the one that wins,
Is the one who thinks he can.

(Author unknown)

1
Lace: then, now and for ever

These are the reminiscences of a past era; so far past, that life for this particular person has come full circle. The experiences of a small child are made vivid by smell, or something one sees, maybe something happens. These same experiences in later life recall and perhaps enhance and exaggerate the memory, and can transport one back to a time that once was. This is what this story is about: a store of memories turned into a textbook.

This particular person was Nenia Margeurite Lovesey. There was always lace in my life. Great Grand-Mother – exactly that – Grand Ma'am, the Guru of the family, knew all there was to know about lace. She sat on her chair with her feet on a velvet stool, and just made lace. Not for her the lighting of fires, cleaning of stoves or filling of the hanging oil lamps. Nor did she ever peel a potato or take the pony and trap to the shops for her material. Good Lord, no! The shopkeepers came to her.

To be allowed into her room on 'Buying Day' was sheer bliss. Trays upon trays of the finest threads, pins, ribbons, silks, and rolls of Indian cotton, printed all over with tiny rosebud sprigs. There might have been many other prints, indeed there were, but my heart was set on the rosebuds. They would match the rosebuds already sewn on to my Sunday straw bonnet.

It is such a pity that children are born so small and take so long to reach the height where they are able to peer above table level. Mind you, one does not have to be that tall, when thoughtless tradesmen leave trays of beautiful bone and ivory bobbins on the floor while trying to sell something even more sumptuous to the adults at a higher level. What child would not take the chance of such a favourable position to get her teeth into that milky white substance to find out what it tasted of? I can see a smile creeping over one or two faces as you now remember getting your teeth into my bobbins.

But to return to our little girl in the story. Why then did she have her hands smacked and suffer the indignity of having the girl who worked in the kitchen summoned to take her away? She had only bitten a few bobbins, after all. On thinking back, I see that I did not improve with keeping, unlike the wine or port that was served in crystal glasses after the buying sessions were over. Comments like 'There is nothing like a glass of good port to ensure that only the best merchandise comes to this house' or 'Wilkens' assistant is badly in need of a bar of Sunlight' (soap that was).

And so when playing at 'Buying Days' and overheard to say to my dolls 'There will be no port today until you wash, Wilkens', it was decided that from that day on I was to be banned from the room when adults were being entertained. 'One can never be sure what that child will come out with next; she could be very embarrassing', was the usual comment.

Great Grand-Mother never actually showed me how to wind a bobbin or dress a pillow, or even how to prepare the background material for a piece of lace. It was taken for granted that, as I had watched the process so many times, I should automatically know the right method from the wrong. No one quite managed to get

FIG 1.1 Devonia lace. From the Ann Aldridge collection

around to explaining that I was left-handed. It was easy to wind bobbins and make the correct knot at the neck – I could even wind two bobbins from each end of a piece of thread and get it right – but when used by a right-handed worker the wound thread would never unwind.

I can still hear the echo of 'How many times must one tell you', before being whisked away to the kitchen. There in the kitchen the tears would squeeze through and have to be wiped away on the nearest sleeve. It is still a very vivid memory.

Grandma was never so haughty. She would wipe away the tears, unwind the bobbins, change the thread and the bobbins into the opposite hand and quietly show how to wind with the right hand. Much, much later as a tutor of lace I could recall the difficulty that I had experienced and it made for ease and comfort when I relayed that problem to my students.

When I was born I was christened Nenia Marguerite, but my father always called me Daisy. Daisies were a favourite flower with lacemakers. The proof? There was a ground called '*Marguerite a centre de toile*'; Bedfordshire laces use Marguerites a lot, sometimes as an eight-petalled flower, sometimes using just four petals, worked within circles and in squares. In Needlepoint lace there is the 'Marguerite Filling'. So why, why, did they call me Daisy? Marguerite can never sound hard and cross, but Daisy – well, I ask you!

If you were a fly on the wall listening to a group of lacemakers, you could be forgiven for not understanding what they were talking about. They would be speaking a language all their own. Words like Headings, Footside, Covering Pins, Winkie Pins, Toile, Tallies, Sewings On, Spiders, Pinchain, Picots, Passives and Workers, Legs, Brides, Leaves, Afficots, Cordonet and Cordonette, Couch Threads and Gimps. These and many more are part of the language of lace.

For Bobbin lace the main words and their meanings are:

Workers: a pair of bobbins that weave over and under the other pairs of bobbins.

Passives: the pairs of bobbins the workers weave through. Once the workers weave through the first pair, they are left aside, while another pair of passives are brought into play and the workers work through this pair. In this way the workers travel through all the passives to the end of a row.

Pin Up: when the workers reach the end of the row, the bobbin on the right is placed over the bobbin on the left. This makes one twist. If you place the right over the left again it makes another twist; a pin is then put between the last pair of passives and the workers, into the topmost hole at the side of the pattern. The thread is then taken round the pin and is ready to work back through the passives in the opposite direction to form the second row. The workers are again twisted twice, as before, always right over left, and another pin is inserted in the top uncovered hole on the other side of the pattern.

Torchon: the name of a type of lace which is always worked down along a row of holes placed at a 45 degree angle. If two pairs of bobbins do not cross each other at this correct angle, it is a sure sign that one is the wrong pair.

When you reach an outside edge of a Torchon pattern, you always go back to the pin hole at the highest point not already covered. This could lead you down a 45 degree line of holes either to the right or to the left. But always look for, and go back to, the highest point unworked.

Torchon lace is the easiest of all the laces to work and can look very pretty if the large patterns are reduced in size and a fine thread used, in keeping with the size of the pattern. Have the designs reduced by photocopying; that way nothing is missed from the original pricking.

Pricking: the name given to a bobbin lace pattern. At first, parchment was used and each pricking kept within a family, passed down from one generation to another. Later, a hard, glazed card was brought into use when lace classes started. Now it is easier to get a photocopy of the pricking, cover it with matt acetate film and *Copydex* it to a firm piece of card. The acetate film stops the photocopy from becoming rubbed and scratched. Once stuck to the card it gives a substantial pricking that will last for ages.

The instructions for working a braid will come first, then those for Torchon ground. After that you must wait for a birthday or Christmas and ask for *The Technique of Bobbin Lace*. If bobbin lace is to become your favourite type of lace, the next book is *The Book of Bobbin Lace Stitches*. This book will help you to draw up your own designs, and will give you a large range of stitches to experiment with.

If only I could have been given such a choice!

Before continuing with the story it would be advisable to know a little about bobbin lace. First of all you need a pillow. This is not like the pillow you have on your bed, but a firm-filled, hard object into which pins can be stuck. There are lots of suppliers who

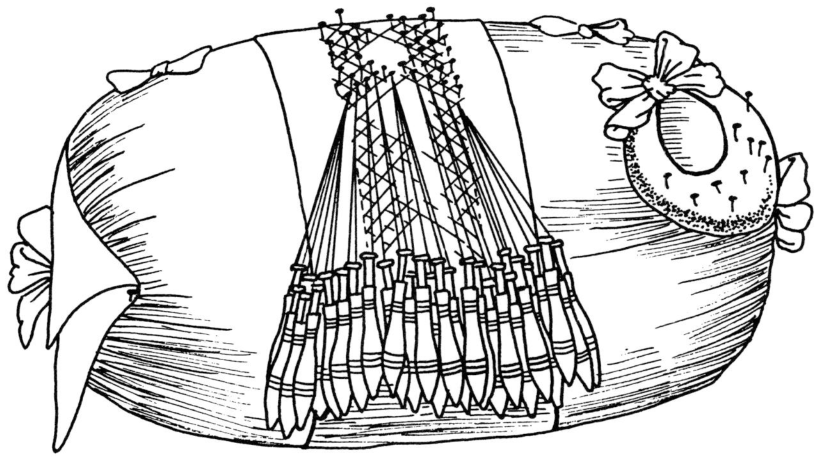

FIG 1.2 A lace pillow

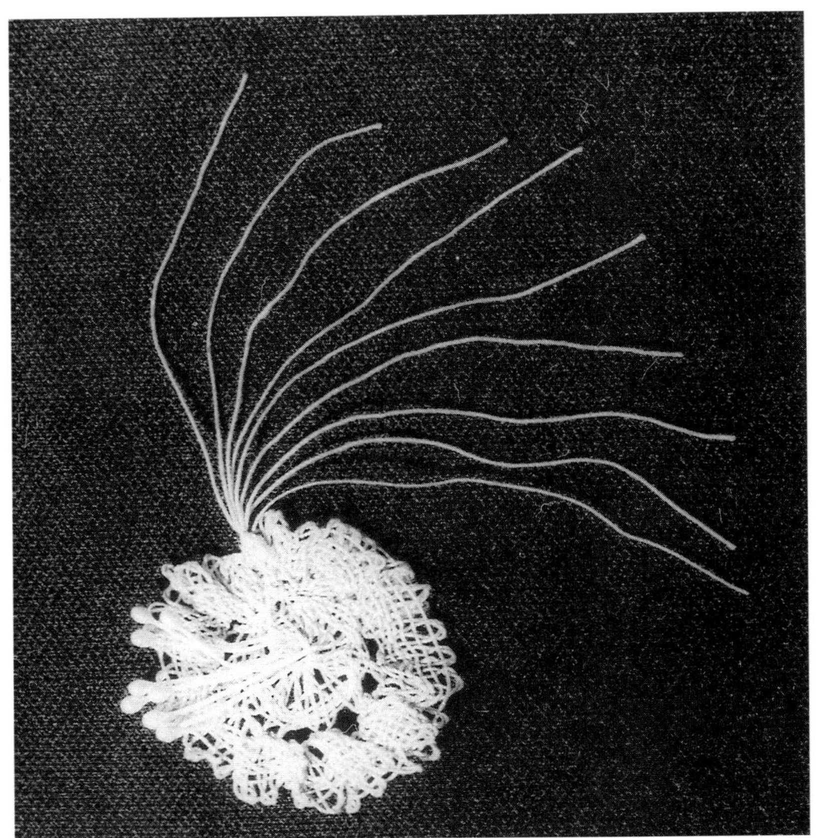

FIG 1.3 Nena Maria's first flower, worked when she was five and given to her mother as a bookmark

produce really well-made pillows and the drawing (Fig. 1.2) shows an old-fashioned type used 60 years ago, not at all like the type you will be expected to use. The photograph (Fig. 2.15) shows the old 'bolster' pillow and pillow 'horse', used nearly a hundred years ago. The 'flash' was the only form of light available before gas and electricity came into use. When there were a few hundred bobbins to be wound, a winder was essential. They are shown in Fig 2.14, and are taken from my own collection. The chair that they stand with is shown in the book by Thomas Wright, *The Romance of the Lace Pillow*.

A lace pillow was always properly 'dressed'. The pin cushion was securely pinned on the right-hand side, ready for the worker's hand (always provided the worker was right-handed: change the position to the other side if you are left-handed).

On the opposite side was a small pocket for holding extra threads or bobbins. At the back of the cushion (pinned across the paper pattern) lies a wider pocket. This is used to hold the lace, keeping it clean and out of the way.

In order to simplify the instructions for making a braid, the bobbins are dealt with in pairs. It is not the bobbins that are numbered, but the places in which the bobbins lie. These places are numbered 1, 2, 3 and 4.

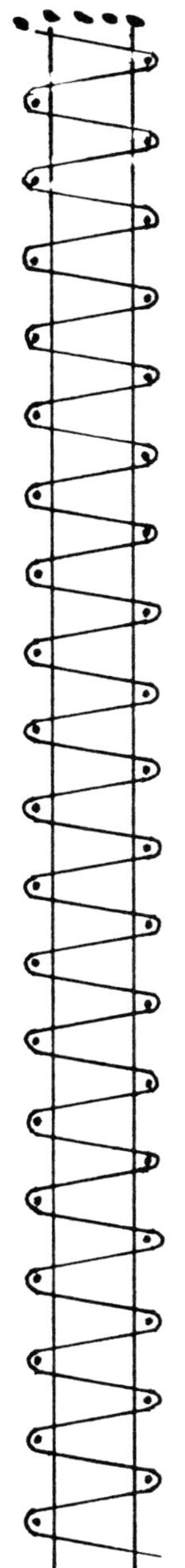

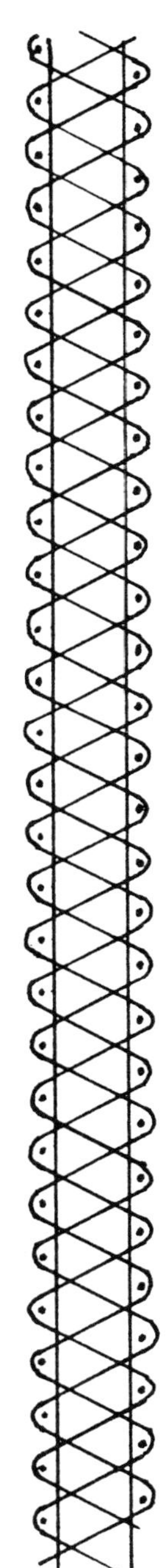

FIG 1.4 Two bobbin lace prickings. The first using a cloth stitch, the second worked in Torchon ground

Whichever bobbin happens to land on whichever place, it takes on that number. For instance, a bobbin will lie in place 1 but will cross over the bobbin in place 2, which turns it into bobbin No 2, and the bobbin in place 2 will have become bobbin No 1.

The first stitch you learn is the linen stitch, using four bobbins.

You place

> bobbin in place 2 over bobbin in place 3
> bobbin in place 2 goes over the one in place 1
> the bobbin lying in place 4 goes over the one in place 3
> the bobbin lying in place 2 now goes over the one in place 3

That sounds very complicated but:

> put 2 over 3
> now pick up 2 and 4 and put them over one bobbin each
> into places 1 and 3
> now put 2 over 3 again

Leave the two bobbins on the left, and take two bobbins from the right, and repeat the stitch again, through this new pair. Continue in the same way through the rest of the pairs.

This may sound odd, but whether you are working from left to right or right to left the movements are always in the same sequence.

If you try to use colour to mark your bobbins, don't expect them to remain in the right order.

The *workers* are the pair that travel across the pairs that hang straight down, which are called the *passives*. The workers can be wound with a different coloured thread, to distinguish them from the other pairs.

The pattern you work from is called a *pricking*. This is a substantial card with pin pricks which mark the pattern. The more even the distance between the holes, the more regular the lace will be when made.

The pins are always placed in the holes in such a manner as to divide the four threads into pairs, the pins being in front of the threads. This is always the case, no matter which stitch is being worked. Dressmaker's pins are best for little hands, but real lace pins, which are very fine, will be necessary as you progress and become more proficient. The trouble is these fine pins do bend under pressure from small hands (and from some big ones too!).

Lace cannot be worked without some type of tool. Needlepoint lace is worked with a sewing needle, Tambour lace needs a tambour hook, and Tatting needs a shuttle. We are dealing with Bobbin lace, so we will need bobbins. Later on, you will work with many, many bobbins at a time; right now we will settle for just one dozen. That will give you ten *passives*, which hang straight down, and two workers which will travel from one side of your lace to the other.

To wind your bobbins, start winding by holding the end of the thread under your thumbnail tight on the neck of the bobbin. Keeping a tight tension on the thread wind round and round until there is about a metre of thread wound neatly on the neck only. Do not cut the thread immediately; unwind another metre, then cut off. Starting at the cut end, wind the second bobbin until there is about 16 cm between the two bobbins.

Now comes the tricky part of the proceedings – that is, the slip

FIG 1.5 Kate Marie at the age of three

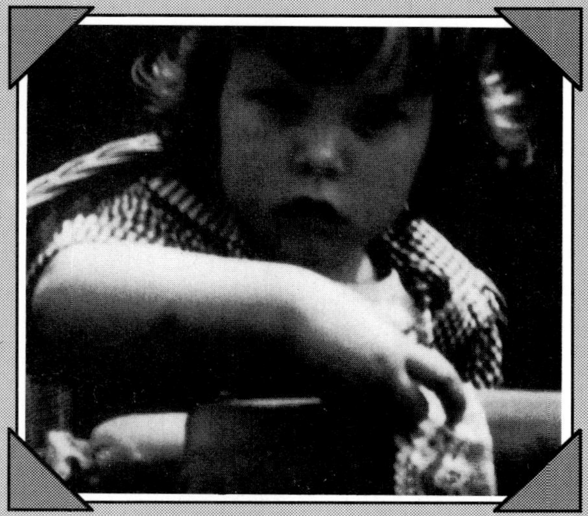

When Kate Marie caught the lace fever in 1981.

First, it's all this	*CONCENTRATION.*
Next is all about	*DETERMINATION.*
Then it has to be	*CONFIGURATION.*
Maybe, even could be	*REALISATION.*
But it is definitely	*EXALTATION.*

and it really doesn't hurt.

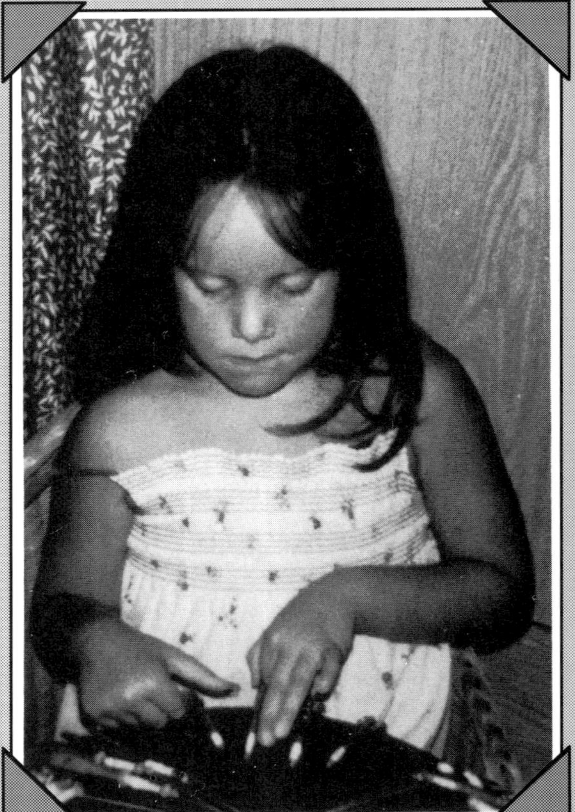

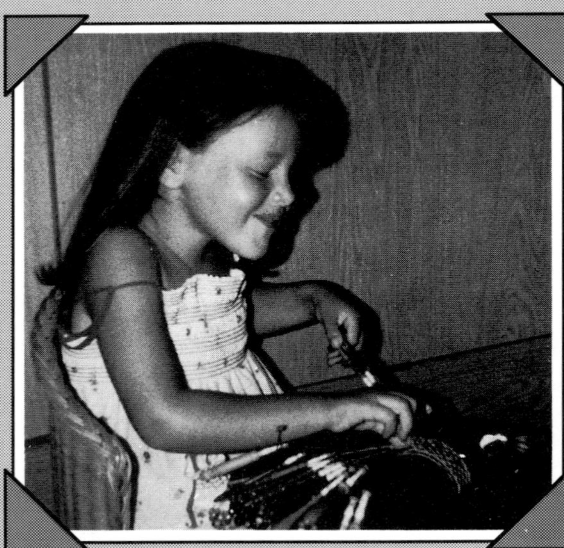

*Three years later it is still Concentration,
Determination, and the correct hand Manipulation,
best of all is the great smirk of Graduation.*

knot that stops the bobbin from unwinding. A loop is made by laying the thread over that coming straight off the bobbin, then slipping the loop over the head of the bobbin. This will only unwind when the bobbin is held sideways; a finger from the other hand holds the thread down on to the pillow, while the bobbin is unwound away from the pillow.

This is just about the spot in the story where I was in trouble for not doing this the right way round.

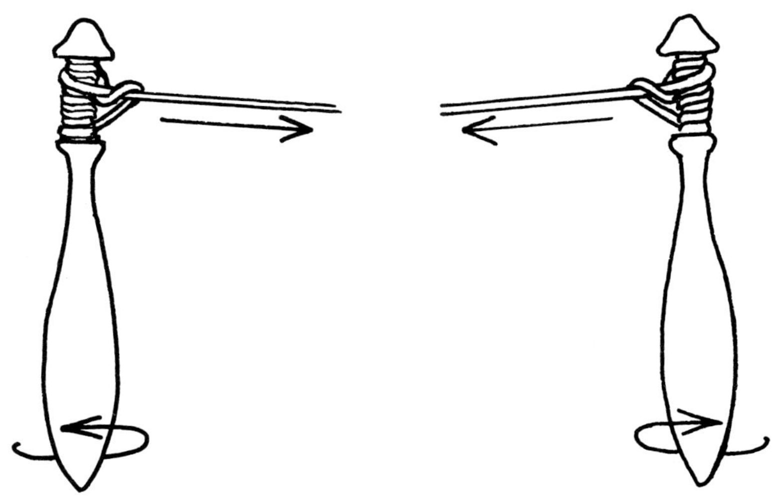

FIG 1.7 Bobbins with the left- and right-handed twist

Fig 1.8 shows a pricking for Torchon Ground. It is worked diagonally, two pairs of bobbins being required for each pin hole. The stitch consists of half a stitch, a pin being put in the hole between the pairs, then another half a stitch to enclose the pin. When that has been done, twist each pair of bobbins twice.

To work the diagram twelve pairs of bobbins are needed. Hang three pairs at the end holes numbered 1 and 5. Hang two pairs at each of the other holes numbered 2, 3 and 4.

Twist the two end pairs three times each, and twist the pair next to each of these twice. Twist the other eight pairs once.

With right-hand pair from 2 and left-hand pair from 1, make a half stitch (2 over 3, 2 over 1 and 4 over 3), put in a pin at hole 6 between the pairs, then enclose the pin by making another half stitch. This leaves each pair twisted once.

Now make the Torchon Edge as follows. Bring the third pair from the outside through the next pair in whole stitch. Twist the right-hand pair once and the left-hand pair twice. Put a pin in hole 7 between pairs but do not enclose.

With the two pairs at the edge make a whole stitch, twist the outside pair three times and the other pair once, then enclose the pin (no. 7) by a whole stitch made with the pairs on each side of it.

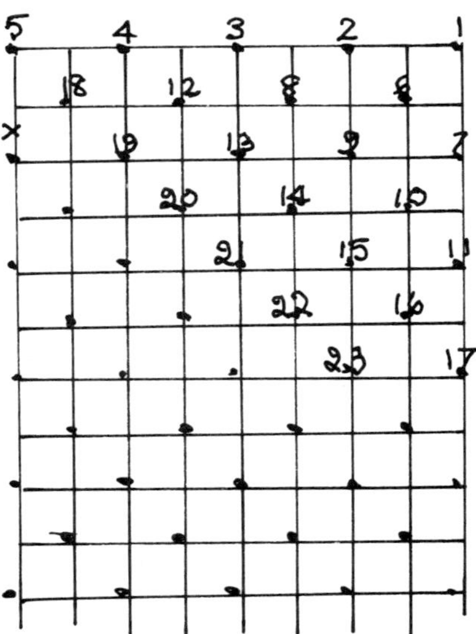

FIG 1.8 Torchon ground

Twist the right-hand pair twice and the left-hand pair once.

Now continue the Torchon Ground. With the right-hand pair from 3 and the left-hand pair from 2, make a half stitch, pin in at 8, enclose it with a half stitch, drop the left-hand pair and pick up the pair from hole 6 to make a stitch in the same way as for hole 9.

Make the other holes in the same way.

Always starting at the highest hole and working down on a 45-degree angle to the end of line and at the end making an edge stitch, continue the rows in succession until hole 25 is complete.

The pair from hole 18 is used to make the left-hand edge stitch at x, worked just as the reverse of the right-hand edge stitch.

Hindu Proverb

Pitiful is the one who, fearing failure, makes no beginning.

2

To London
to find a Knight

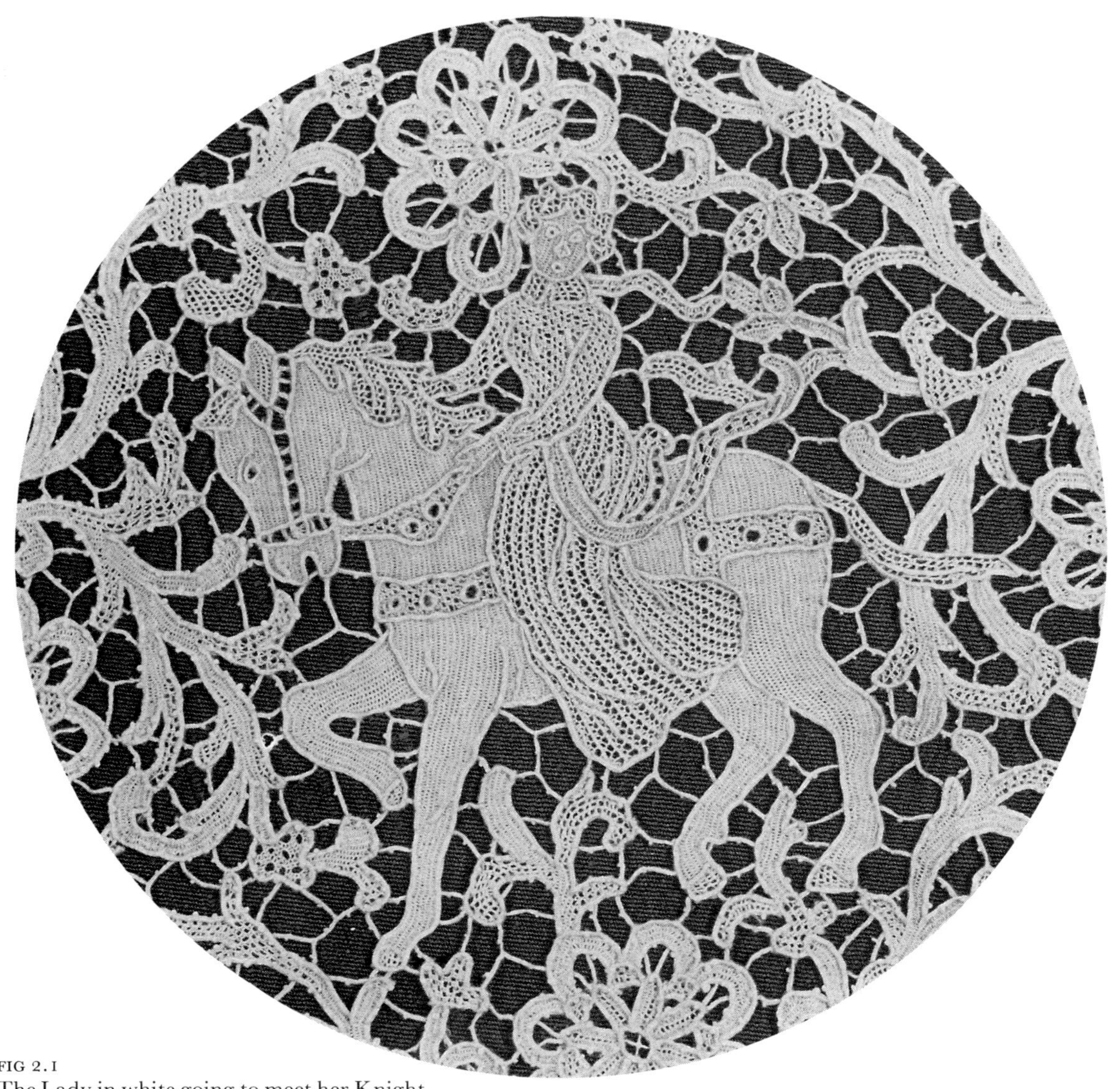

FIG 2.1
The Lady in white going to meet her Knight
Her Knight in shining armour.
She met her dream, is now the Lady in green
And her Knight has rusty armour.

FIG 2.2 When working a design of
this sort, follow the contours of
the bodies. Make sure that the
faces and hands recede by
working the outline of the clothes
with the 'head' of the buttonhole
stitch overlying the features

FIG 2.3 If the stitch tension is
tight, the overall design will be
slightly smaller when removed
from the backing material

FIG 2.4 & 2.5 Features need a
smooth surface, the easiest stitch
to work evenly is the Corded
Bruxelles. The costumes and
leaves can be worked in a variety
of stitches. Do try to work some
shading into the design following
the instructions on page 31 in
Creative Design for Needlepoint Lace

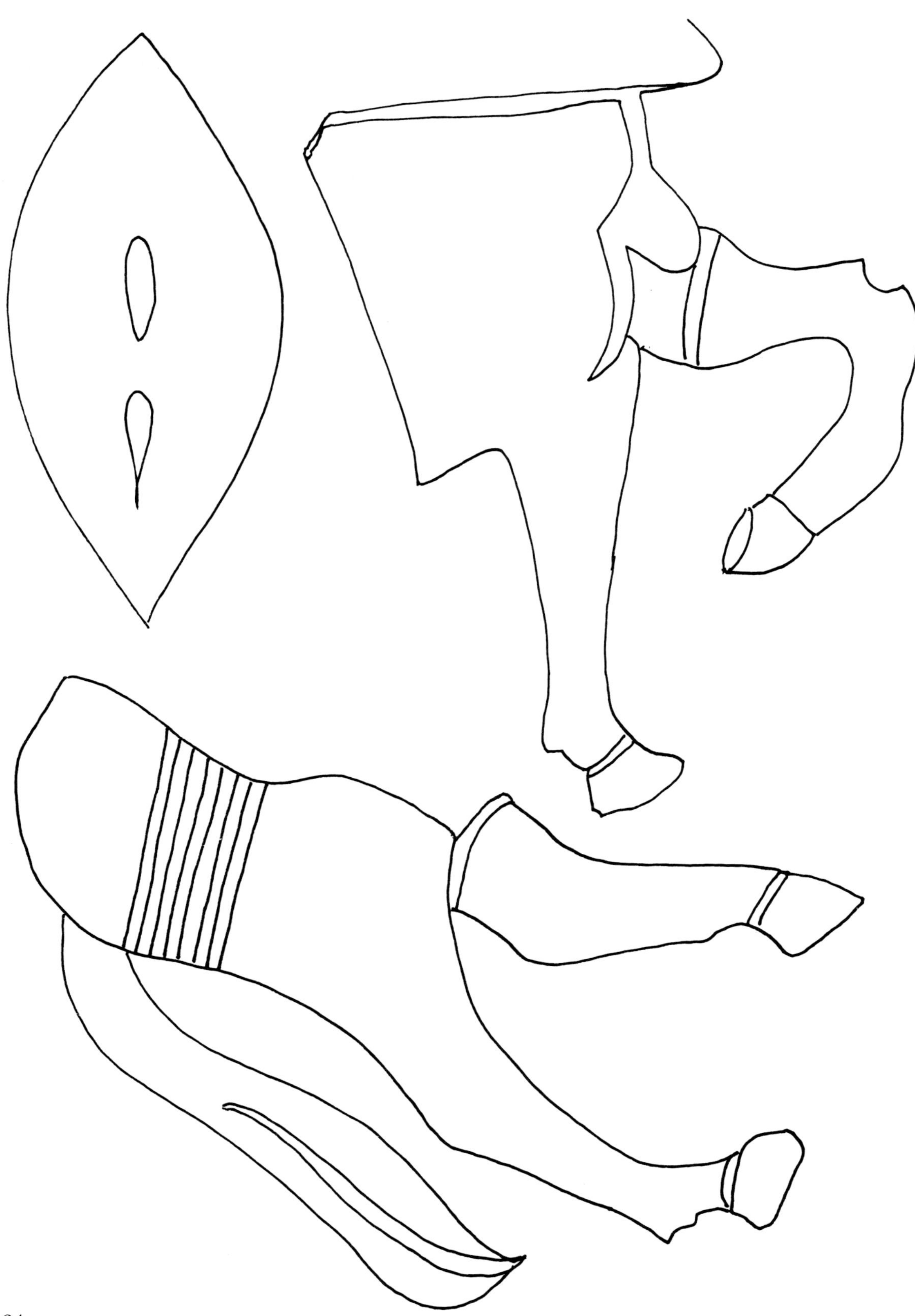

When I was aged about four, the highlight of my year was to travel up from Devon to stay with Paternal Grandparents while Mother taught for two weeks at the school of Louisa and Rosa Tebbs. The school was a tall house that reached to the sky, in Kensington Church Street in London. There was a basement where meals were served, then there were winding stairs that went right to the top, so high up the windows were turrets, because by the time one reached the top, the house had become a castle. One could see for ever and ever over the roof-tops. This was where the lace for grand ladies was kept. I was sure that one day a Knight in shining armour would climb all those stairs to choose a laced handkerchief for his Lady. It seemed a pity he never arrived while I was there, because I had never seen a Knight before.

By the time I had reached the top everyone would be hunting for that errant child, and, once found, I would be expected to be seen but not heard until one of the staff took me to see 'Albert'. He was a funny stone man at the top of a lot of steps. Not the same warm wood stairs, twisting and curling all the way to the top of the house in Church Street; these steps were cold stone, straight and grazed my knees. But adults were under the impression that running up and down the steps a couple of times would make me hungry or tired – hopefully both.

One year in particular, there was to be an exhibition of the Tebbs lace in America. To keep me out of the drawing-rooms where the classes were being held, I was taken down to the basement. There I sat on a long trestle table where all the exhibits were being laid in blue tissue paper and put into strong boxes ready for their long journey over the sea. Each box was carefully labelled, and each label written in ink in the most gorgeous copperplate handwriting. It was there and then that I decided to become an artist. For just one moment the design was more important than the lace. It only lasted one moment, as pandemonium broke out. Labels were missing; everyone began talking at once. There were cries of 'Yes they were here', and 'I remember writing them', and 'Somebody has moved them'. Things began to get out of hand, it all became a little fraught and it was decided that this was no place for a little girl. I was lifted off the trestle table only to reveal the labels stuck to my hot little legs. I went around for the rest of the day with copperplate handwriting on my not-so-clean white knickers, and across the tops of my legs. Now the only way I could admire the little works of art was to stand with my back to one of the many long mirrors, bend in half and look through my legs. Found in this position by one of the tutors, my bottom was sharply smacked for being so unladylike. What a waste of lovely writing when one could not even read it – not that I could read, to me it was just a pretty design.

Another thing that was most unfair, was that at four o'clock the classes would end and all the ladies would have tea and cakes, oozing with cream, just waiting to drop on their pillows or needlepoint. I was not allowed to have a cake because it would make my hands sticky, even though I was not making lace. Grown-ups were most unreasonable; there was Madeira or seedcake in the basement if I was hungry. Little did 'they' know how sticky hands could get rolling Madeira cake into little balls to throw out of the window to the sparrows.

A favourite game that I played while at the school was pretending to be invisible. All the tables in the drawing rooms were round, polished and had pedestal legs. Large white, lace-edged cloths covered the tables and these cloths almost touched the ground. The game was to crawl slowly into one of the rooms, hide under a table and make funny faces at myself in the patent leather shoes covering the feet of the ladies sitting at the table. Mummy knew about this invisible act, but kept it a secret, because it kept me quiet all through tea break. I was sure that Miss Rosa knew about it too, because she would lift the corner of a cloth to try to catch me out. This made the game more exciting because I had to reach the table furthest away from the tutor and Miss Rosa without being seen by anyone.

It was also wonderful to get into the rooms before the classes started, to try to work out how the patterns for the lace on the cloths was made. The only lesson in needlepoint lace that I ever really had was one morning after being caught 'studying' the lace. Miss Louise came in to give the room a final glance before the ladies arrived and found me trying to draw the pattern formed by the holes in the lace. Miss Louise said drawing in that position was most uncomfortable and that I should go up to her office where she would find me some real drawing paper and pencils. That was the first time I had ever been told that an HB pencil should be used for drawing the outlines of a design and an H or hard pencil should be used to draw the fine filling stitches. I was even shown how to draw the thread to make it look as if it was laying under another piece of thread. Being an inquisitive child, I wanted to know how the holes held together in the lace background and I was very serious about it all. Miss Louise found all the necessary things and showed me how to pull the second thread in from the edge of a piece of tape. This pulled the tape up to go round corners. It was also explained that the inferior, machine-made tape could not do this and that one had to run in a thread to gather up. It was also a way in which a small girl could tell the difference between hand-made lace and that made by machine. It was explained that machine lace was woven so that the edges were locked by the weaving and therefore could not pull up into a gather. Machine lace was always referred to as 'that stuff', so you could see that it was instilled into me at a very early age that hand-made lace was the real thing.

When enough tape had been pulled up, it had to be sewn on to a piece of soft kid leather that had a squiggly line to follow. All this hard work had to be done before the stitches could be worked.

I settled down for the rest of the morning trying hard to make small stitches as fast as Miss Louisa could. One lesson learned that morning was that small stitches took ages to work, but large ones had to be unpicked. Another lesson learned the hard way was that a thimble stopped a hole forming in the top of a finger. The trouble

FIG 2.6 This design is being worked with the very narrow braid used for Branscombe Lace, and Metler 30 thread in black, white and shades of grey

was that when the thimble was on the middle finger I pushed the needle through with the fourth finger until that had a hole in it. When I put the thimble over that hole I used the middle finger till that had a hole in it too.

By then it was time to go and see Albert, but my keeper met a soldier on the way (this often happened) so the pigeons were fed instead.

That first piece of tape lace turned out to be dreadful. It was thick, and by the time it was finished it was filthy, so I decided tape lace was not my forte. My lace would be the dainty white lace that the ladies were being taught.

This news was relayed to Miss Rosa who said that in future I could sit in the drawing rooms, could listen, watch and take notice, but was not to touch or talk or interfere in any way. It was sheer bliss and I was able to learn more that way than by attending any classes as a student.

I wonder if Albert missed his morning visit from Daisy? And I wondered why I was never allowed to sit in my mother's class.

I was never told about pattern design, the basics or the vocabulary – these things had to wait until I went to art college. Many of you are ready to make that grade and I hope will go on to bigger and better things, so the next few pages should help. First the vocabulary, then some drawings to start off with.

Abstract: separated from matter. An ideal way or a theoretical way of regarding things.

Counterchange: this is working on a pattern that has roughly equal quantities of two contrasting colours or textures. The lines between the two form the boundaries; either quantity can be the figure or the background. This is also called 'Figure Ground Reversal'.

Negative space: if one of the colours or textures were taken away from the design mentioned above, it would leave a negative space. In other words, it is the background or empty space. In needle lace, when two designs placed side by side leave a space, it is called a casket. These spaces should be studied very closely because they are often as interesting as the original design.

Diaper: a term often used in weaving. It is the pattern that forms when the headles are moved in the same repeat mode. This applies to lace when the line of each unit forms part of the outline for the next unit. Alençon lace was made in this way. Each worker specialised in one particular unit of the design. All units were then brought together to be joined in the same way as a jigsaw would be put together.

Repeat: a design composed of two or more identical elements.

Mirror Image: where one element is drawn in reverse. To do this the original design is turned over and traced off, either by holding the design up to a window or by using a light box. The mirror image and the original design then form the repeat.

Unit: the basic shape that can be repeated as a complete unit of a design.

Interlace: a linear pattern; perhaps tape lace would be the best example, where the design passes over and under a continuous line producing a complex Turk's Head Knot effect. The best known example is the Celtic Illuminated Manuscripts, the most famous of these being the *Book of Kells*, now in the library of Trinity College, Dublin, Ireland.

Scale: the relative or proportionate size. Any design given in a book can be enlarged or reduced. Related to this is the appropriate size of thread that would have to be used to compensate. The bigger the reduction, the finer the thread, the bigger the enlargement, the thicker the thread.

Scroll: an ornamental design, especially in architecture, carved or drawn to imitate a scroll of parchment, more or less exactly. Copies of the anthology *Knights Scroll Ornaments* are held in some museums; Dover Publications have a condensed version that is very useful.

Grid or Net Lines: the lines of any network, also a skeleton of a pattern on which a design can be built.

Out of context: taking something out of its original surroundings (which give it meaning) and using it in a different way that is deliberately misleading.

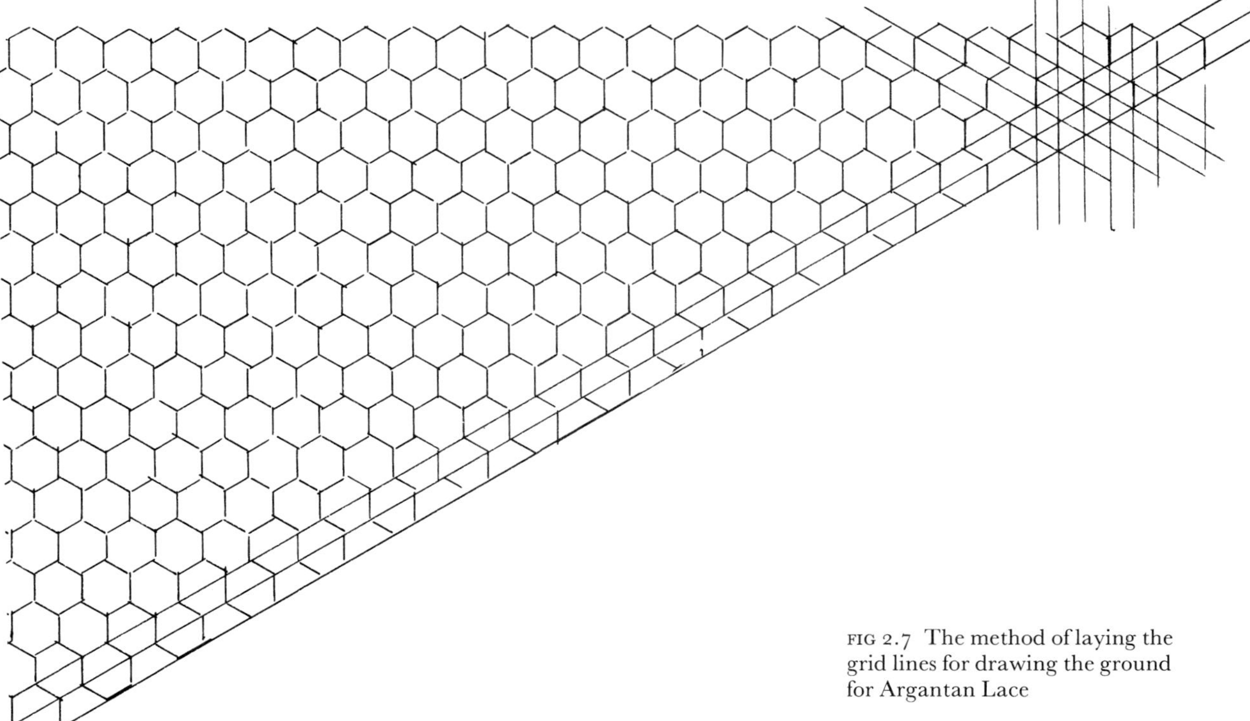

FIG 2.7 The method of laying the grid lines for drawing the ground for Argantan Lace

FIG 2.8 The finished grid. The
method of working this ground is
given on page 83 in *The Technique
of Needlepoint Lace*

Now the Shapes. There are only a limited number of shapes, yet they have unlimited possibilities. The following will give you enough ideas to make you think for a while: the *circle*, an *oval*, a *square*, the *ogee*, the *egg*, or *tear-drop*, to name the obvious. Let us take a limited number of ways for each of these.

The circle will give scope for counterchange. It can be laid on a grid to form a pattern, or interlaced, one with another (or others such as the Olympic Games symbol), laid in an overlapping formation in various scrolls, halved and laid open end up to form scallops, or into a circle or half moon shape with the open end facing in or out. Each way will suggest different uses and different designs.

The oval, halved along the centre of its longest axis, gives an enclosed elliptical shape that can form the basis of many designs. This can be halved again to give curves. Using an oval in the shape of an egg gives an asymmetrical shape because one end is narrower, thus giving a sweeping curve that can be mirror-imaged to give a good outline.

The square can be many things. It can be used in brick formation and the half drops used as when designing for wallpaper. Turn it on end and it becomes a diamond. Diamonds can be halved to become triangles. Any of these can be used as grids or net-lines, for counterchange or figure reversal. Squares used in any of these ways can be used as intervals or as a space between recurring elements. They can be filled with a circle or a square within a square, forming a diamond, or alternate blocks of solid stitches against openwork areas.

The ogee can be used in block formation or singularly as a main shape. Again, many of the things already mentioned work well if the ogee is used as a grid. Counterchange, filled with circles, ovals, blocked as spaces, or leaving four empty units and filling the surrounding areas with solid stitches. Used for stitch samplers by filling each unit with different stitches, it makes a pleasant change from the usual squares.

The hexagon works in the same way as the ogee; in fact two samplers worked with identical stitches can look completely different because, overall, the stitches lie in other directions and so take on another appearance. These last two shapes make the most interesting grids to work on when experimenting with colour.

The tear-drop, whether real tears, a dripping tap, or frozen icicles, can change its shape the nearer it gets to the ground, because of the pull of gravity. The shape can be almost oval, changing to pear shape, and the end can even curl to one side very slightly. Try watching a very slow drip from a tap, or raindrops running down a window-pane.

Water can produce some of the most exciting designs. Lie in a bath of bubbles and watch how they cling together for a while, then as some burst they divide into shapes, areas of water appear, and colours abound in every bubble but constantly change and disappear. It is not easy to draw in the bath, as the paper gets very sodden. It is much better to take a photograph. Fill the kitchen sink

FIG 2.9 & 2.10 Machine lace has
been used to illustrate this
particular exercise. Since the
thread is so fine and the design so
intricate it makes an interesting
example of counterchange or
figure reversal

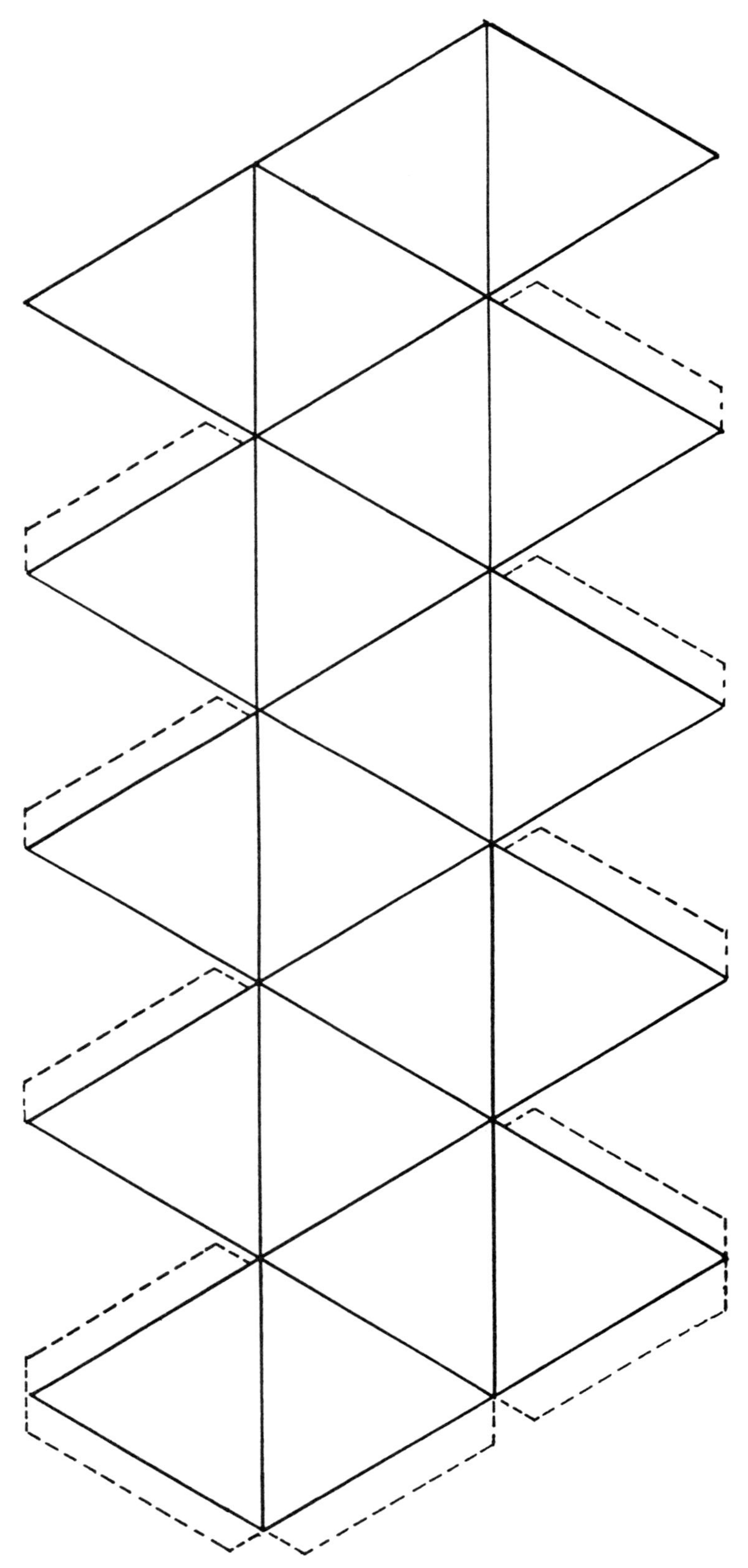

FIG 2.11 Triangles placed in such
a way that they form a ball when
all edges are sewn together

FIG 2.12 (1) Scale units in conventional network design; (2) Paired scale units; (3) The ogee is based on the S-bend and can be used vertically, horizontally or stretched into graceful curves; (4) Forming the ogee. Draw a square or rectangle and within the framework draw a diamond, then the St George and St Andrew crosses. The four S-bends are drawn around this grid

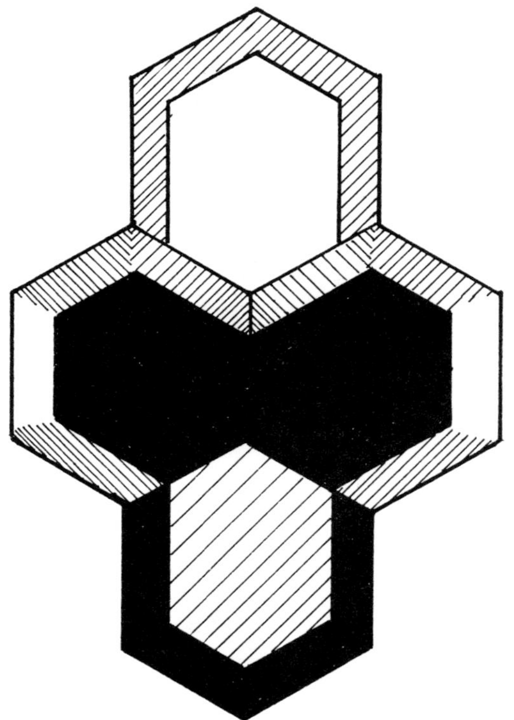

FIG 2.13 Playing with the hexagon

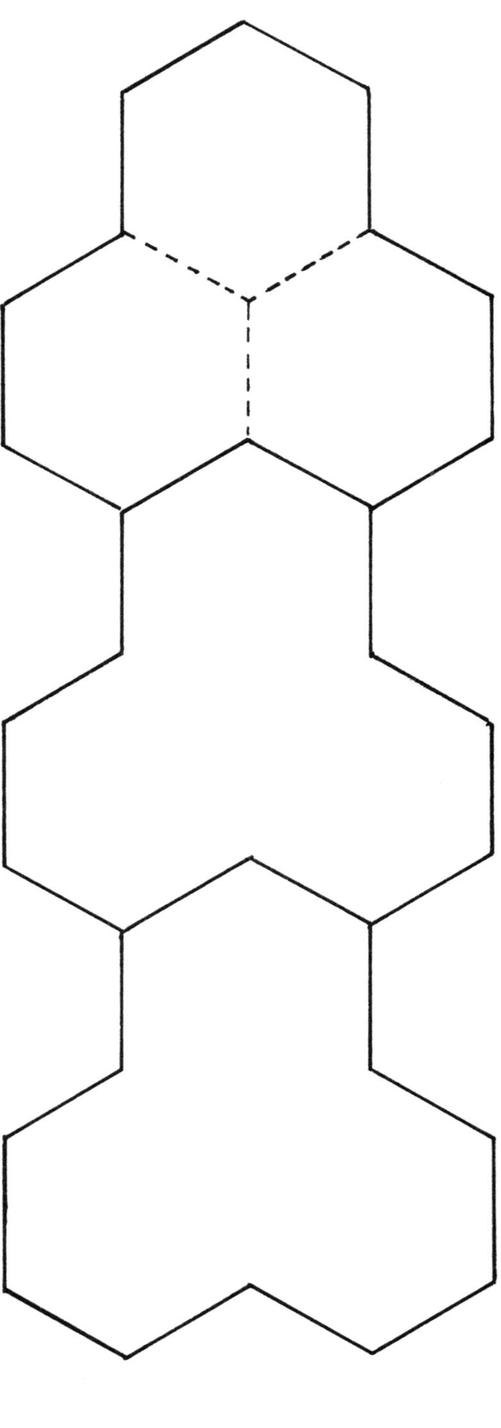

FIG 2.14 Flash, bobbin winder, spool holder, together with the pattern sampler book that belonged to the Winslow Lace Association

with warm water, dissolve a little liquid soap, add a few drops of vegetable dye and then pull the plug out. The water will run away anti-clockwise, driving the foam and colours around with it. It all moves away too quickly to sketch, but one or two photographs will give you many ideas.

So will the sea. Stand on top of stones looking down from a jetty or harbour wall, or watch the ripple of water as each wave trickles back across the sand, or the big sea horses when it is rough – that is when you see Venetian lace. Find a clump of stones, large ones, where the sea has formed a shallow pool that does not dry out when the tide recedes. There you will find asymmetric designs already laid out for you. Given shape, colour, and texture all in one place, you can sit and draw till the tide comes in without once getting your paper wet.

Frozen water and heavy frosts abound with designs. Have you ever stopped and studied a blackberry bush or bracken after a hoar-frost? Two or three photographs will give plenty of inspiration. Now you will begin to realise why photography is included in art courses and in City and Guild exams.

Do you know what reminds me of lace? A spider's web on a frosty morning. There it hangs, pristine white, crisp but exquisite, detailed but so dainty and very precarious and insecure. You will know what I mean by insecure when you have dropped a pillow or two. You will understand precarious after you have lived with lace and children. Pristine white? Not your first pieces, I can guarantee you that, but it will not be long before your work is dainty – after that comes 'exquisite', and that is what real lace is.

This was the type of lace first made in Venice, and much valued on account of the beauty of its design. The Church and the Court vied with each other to see which could own the most valued pieces. It was hoarded away with other jewels, such was its price. In the twentieth century there is no possibility of you becoming materially rich in money because you can make this, the most beautiful of all laces. The satisfaction and pride you will feel once you have mastered the making of it will make you feel rich, that's all. Soon I will no longer be able to instruct the younger ones of our clan but there is also a very happy thought. You will all grow up knowing of Cathy Barley and if your work reaches her standard I will be over the moon with all of you. Leonardo di Vinci once said 'Poor is the student who does not surpass his master'. Well, I was Cath's master and she has produced work far superior to anything I can do now, so into her hands go all my Granddaughters. The lesson here is that if each attains the very highest standards, this lace will never die out. There will always be lace in this family.

'And gladly wolde he lerne,
and gladly teche'

so said the Clerk in the Prologue to the Canterbury Tales.

From **Mr. Thomas Wright.**

COWPER SCHOOL,

OLNEY, BUCKS.

5 Dec 1919

To Mrs H. A. Rae Hubbard

Dear Madam

Thank you for your very kind letter & cheque. I am sorry there are a few slips in the book but these shall be rectified in the 2nd edition, which I hope the war will reach.

Yours faithfully

Thomas Wright

Cowper School,
Olney, Bucks,
6 July 1919

Dear Madam

I am returning with many thanks the book of specimens of lace. I sent 18 headlines & think the taking very hard by some of the workers doing in the school, & the photographer has over-lit on the picture required. I am so very much obliged to you for helping me.

Yours faithfully

Thomas Wright.

Worker	Can make these no.s of lace	Name	Remarks
Mrs Barton	85 a	Greek border	Not well enough to do any.
"	24	Insertion Leaf Motif	
Mrs Sarah Sirett	63 a	Greek Insertion	Dead.
"	45 a	Rose Insertion	
Mrs Thomas Phillips	78	Russian Spider	Would like to do a little
"		Milanese Collar	
Mrs Thomas White	21	Jubilee border	Dead
" John Sirett	21 a	" Insertion	Willing to do some later on
Fanny White	22	Maltese Doyleys	Gone away
Jane Giles	14	Palestrina	Dead .
Mrs Henry Phillips	43 a	Tiny Squares	Dead
" " "	44 a	" Pines	
" " "	86	Russian Union	
" " "	26 c	New Maltese Appligue	
" " "	9	Old Italian	
Kate Phillips	61	Narrow Greek Ins:	Cannot do any at present
" "	8½	Torchon edging	
Mrs Jabez "	8	" border	Would like to do some.
" Jessie Sirett	52	Cluny Insertion	Not well enough to do any
" Samuel Phillips	12	Guipure Squares	Not at present.
" Arthur "	55 a	Tiny Daisy border	Would like to do some
" John "	55 a	" " "	Dead
" G Corbett	53	Little Maltese Ins =	Would like to do some.
" "	41 a	Bakers edg.	
" "	1 a	Easter border	
" "	1 a a	" Ins:	
" John Clarke		Perugia border	Gone away.
Mrs Harry Corbett			Would like to do some.

End of the Windsor Lace Industry
June 1925

FIG 2.16 Papers from the
Winslow (Bucks) Lace Industries,
that sadly ended in 1925. From
the Author's collection

FIG 2.17 A polyhedron made of
different faces

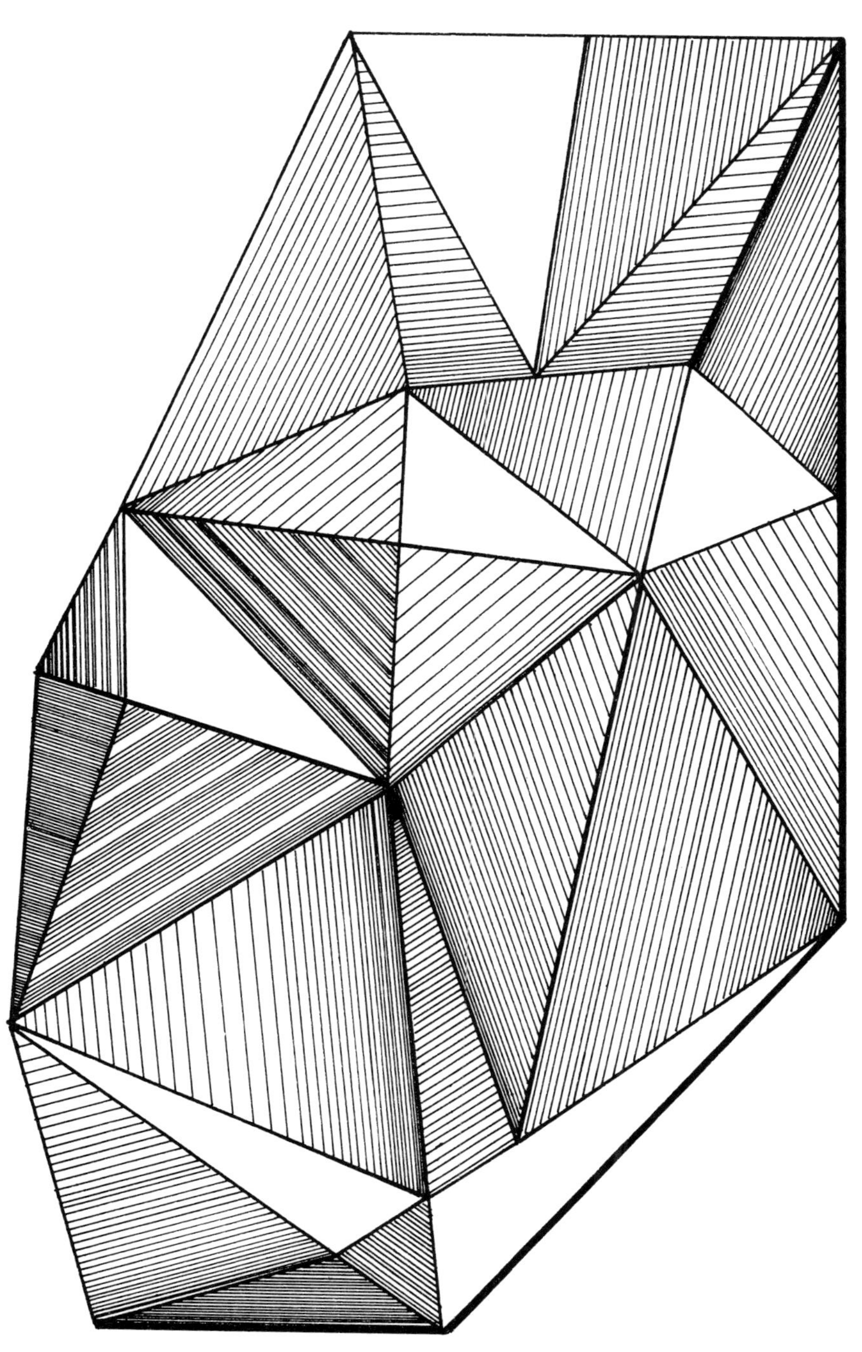

The forgotten language of shapes

This is purely for those of you who at some stage might become involved with making lace for the Church or in restoration of Vestments. When you know what the shapes mean, it makes the work so much more interesting. Be careful how you place the shapes together if using them for stitch samplers – you might. be saying the wrong thing.

How many of you know that the Triangle, or Pythagorean, is a symbol of wisdom? It is also the triple personality of God. Back in the age of the sign, before the written characters, some joker decided that the triangle, standing firmly on one full side, symbolised the female, while if it was standing on its apex it was the male element. The definition then was that the female had an earthly conception, while the male was celestial. Thinking about it, the woman has two feet on the ground, while the man walks around unsure of himself, waiting to topple over.

So we take the two triangles and stand them so that they touch each other at their apex, two whole figures as yet neither damaged nor interfered with, and they form an egg-timer. When the male element falls, as it surely must standing as it does, and passes through the female element, we have a star. Look at that star carefully: there is the central hexagon, but what about the six little triangles those two triangles have produced?

Wait a moment as we allow those two triangles to get over the starry eyed bit. They continue their own sweet ways and form a square standing on one fragile corner. They have a common base line, but they point away from each other and become two triangles again. Today this sign stands for the Evangelists. Let our triangles topple over and we have a square. This brings us down to earth, for this is the emblem of the world and nature. It is the four elements, the four Evangelists and the Christian emblem of worldliness.

The Pentagram is a five-pointed star, drawn with one stroke of a piece of chalk, as it would have been in those far-off days (or as a continuous line made with a chisel). There are several different histories of man connected with this shape. It is Solomon's seal, the Celtic witch's foot or the goblin's cross of the Middle Ages. It stands for the five senses, the Druid's sign of Godhead; for the Jewish faith it is the five Mosaic Books. It is a sign of safety and a protection against devils or demons. When used as an amulet it was the emblem of a happy home-coming. Maybe it stands for many other things as well.

The Octogram, or eight-pointed star, is again made from one continuous line and has no explanation for its being. As I was born in October, I feel that it just about sums it up for me, too. These three stars are used more times than is realised. If you study the centres of each, you will find the shapes used for patchwork. The intertwined triangles form the six-sided Hexagon. The five-pointed star is the Pentagon, while the eight-pointed star is the Octagon; the Square and the Triangle are also used in patchwork. It is surprising what one learns when embarking on a lace course.

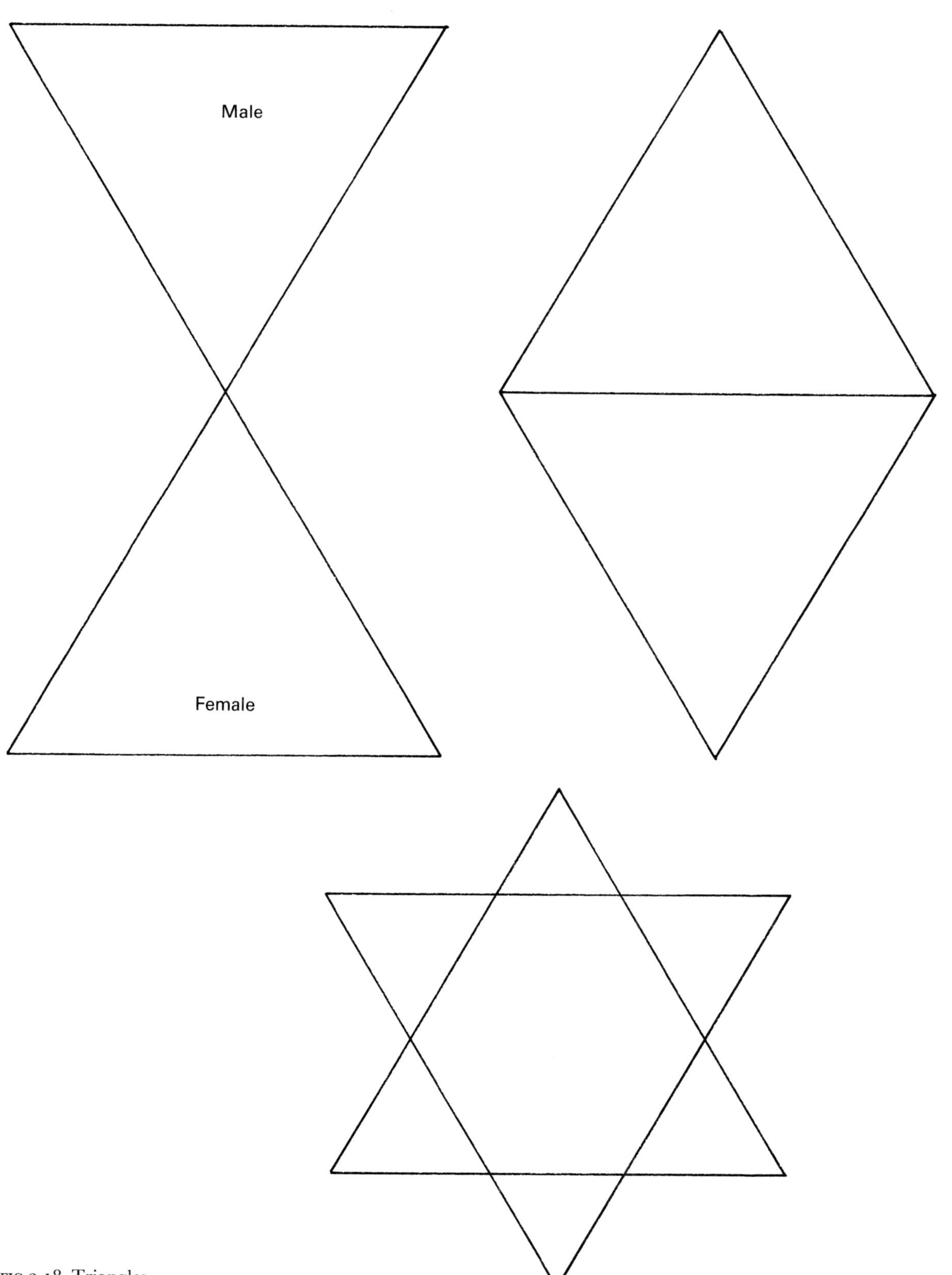

FIG 2.18 Triangles

FIG 2.19 Geometric designs from
basic triangles

FIG 2.20 Tape design

Outlining the design

First measure the length of the design and make sure that you have
enough tape to lay from start to finish. For a repeat pattern such as
the ones given in Fig 2.20 there is only need to measure one repeat,
then multiply by the number of repeats you intend to work. The
larger design will have to be measured from start to finish and the
easiest way to do this is inch by inch round the design. Remember
that the bobbin-made tape will gather if the second thread is pulled
carefully. Do this on both sides of the tape to allow it to follow
curves that go both to the left and to the right.

Once these threads have been pulled through on both sides, tie the ends together so that they cannot slip back; the diagram shows how the design is laid. Curves can be formed with the gathers, but tight corners are best dealt with by folding the tape over at an angle that suits the design. Keep the gathers in the tape running ahead of the design, and carefully ease them back to where they are needed to turn either round to the left or to the right.

Machine-made tape lace can be bought by the metre from most of the suppliers listed at the end of the book. Remember also that this lace has to have a thread run through both sides to gather up. Use a long continuous thread and avoid any knots forming, otherwise the thread will not run through the lace easily.

'Why?', you might ask, 'give instructions for bobbin lace, when the book is essentially about needlemade lace?'

FIG 2.21 Jabot made from bobbin lace tape, some with a Honiton edge, gathered into shape and held in place with herringbone stitches

The answer to that is Branscombe Point. There is a revival of this lace in Devon, thanks to the English Lace School, and as this book is basically a textbook it is important that it be included. Real Branscombe Lace needs a fine, bobbin-made braid; this cannot be bought so it has to be made, hence the instruction. 'Why?', you may then ask, 'give instructions for the Torchon Ground?' Because a fine thread and a Torchon Ground gives a net that your pieces of needlemade lace can be mounted on to. It is more substantial than a half stitch ground and the first pieces of your lace will be too heavy for a flimsy net. (Of course you can always defeat the object and buy machine-made net and braid.)

This is an actual kid pattern that I used long ago. If you look along the footside very carefully, there is a name and a date. The lady who drew the pattern was named Mademoiselle Riego de la Blanchardière. The date is 1868. She was a very versatile lady, because she wrote the *Netting Book for Guipure d'Art* in 1868. She also discovered that a certain type of Spanish lace could be effectively copied in crochet. In about 1846 she published instructions for a few patterns.

When Ireland suffered so badly after the potato famine, these patterns were used by many ladies to teach the work to the farm labourers' wives in order that they could earn a living. In some cases it was the only money the families had to live on. Therefore it is reasonable to say that Mademoiselle Riego invented Irish Crochet Lace.

She continued to write books and to draw designs for lace for the next forty years, but today her name seems to have been forgotten. A very clever lady who should be remembered, and so, my granddaughters, just remember. The piece of tape lace lying beside the pattern was worked in 100 linen thread, using just fourteen bobbins, and has a Honiton edge.

To progress surely, is to go forward slowly, and so the tape becomes part of a design in needlepoint lace. There is only one stitch in needlepoint lace and that is the buttonhole stitch. It is the numerous ways in which this one stitch can be placed that form the different stitch patterns for the designs. From light to heavy, from open to close work, all can be done with this one stitch.

FIG 2.22 Irish crochet, worked over 100 years ago by my Grandmother from a pattern by Mademoiselle Riego de la Blanchardière

48

1. This needlepoint design was worked by Daphne Keen from a bobbin lace pricking

2. Designed and worked by Cathy Barley

3. The Knight and His Lady. Worked by the Author in Gütermann 100/3s silk

4. The Wedding Party. From the Anne Aldridge Collection

5. A Shannon Swan. Worked by Kate Marie in
Crochet Cotton 100

6. The Lily Pond, complete with resident.
Designed and worked by Iris Walbank

7. Siblings. The bonnet and cap
redesigned and worked by the
Author

8. Something To Crow About.
Designed and worked by the
Author in Chinese silks 120/2s

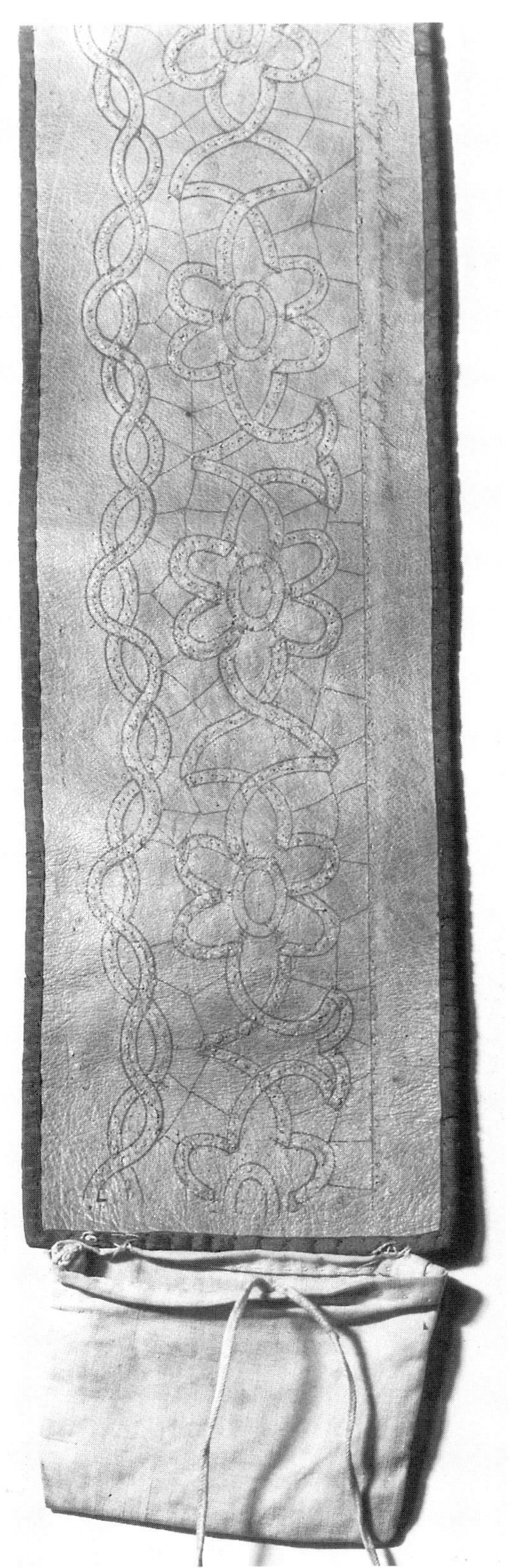

FIG 2.23 Kid tape pattern   FIG 2.24 Tape lace

3

Thoughts of home

In the last we heard of my escapades we were still in Kensington, but all holidays come to an end and it was back home once more. Now, the end of holidays usually means *school*. Like all little girls, I grew older. Suddenly, I was five, and you all know what that means! The horror of it all, sitting at a desk all day, with mind far away thinking of all the things Great Grandmother, Grandma, and Mother would be doing. There would be all those lovely smells: Ashes of Roses talc for sprinkling over hot sticky hands, the smell of bread being baked, the smell of seaweed that had been washed up on the last tide.

Sitting at that horrid little desk, there was only the smell of chalk and a vile smell, which in later years I realised was the smell of dry rot. Then there was the smell of the gas works, not far off; oh, the longing for home. Enough was enough. A bell rang, and the children were sent off to the dining-room; all except one. There was only one place for her, and that was home – to help put away the bobbins, maybe some to be rewound if there was a new lace to be started in the morning. Maybe even better, Mother would be starting on a design for some Princess's ballgown. Every ballgown was for a Princess, each modesty vest was for an old lady. There were never any grown-ups between these two categories, but plenty of Christening robes and baby bonnets.

Very few and far between there would be the flurry of wedding veils, head-dresses and of course the odd parasol. More about one of those later. That was miles away, back home, and on the first day at school, having been taken in the trap and left with nothing but lunch for the day and a threepenny-bit that had been handed in to Teacher for drinks for the rest of the week, how did one get home? Where exactly was home? I had never heard of the word panic, but at that moment I knew what it felt like.

Mother said 'When frightened, never cry; it waters down the brain and stops one thinking properly'. Well, never mind, there was Queen Anne's lace growing in the ditch outside school and it grew all along the lane at home, so getting home was easy, you just followed the Queen Anne's lace. It was quite a shock to find a river in the way. It was very wide in one direction with the sea in the distance in the opposite direction. Home was by the sea, so common sense said I should head in that direction.

There were plenty of boats moored in the mud – well, not so much moored as floored – and it was easy to walk out and sit in one. The logic of this was that all boats owned a fisherman, there was a packet of lunch to eat, so it was just a case of sitting down and waiting for the man of the boat to turn up. Goodness knows what the outcome of that episode would have been but for the ferryman bringing over some fishermen at that point. He knew the cold, frightened child (who had not shed one tear up till then), whisked her over the river and delivered her home. You can guess the rest: a hot, sticky bunch of Queen Anne's lace in one hand, minus a pair of new shoes left behind in the boat on the other side of the river, one smacked bottom and bed. Safe and happy in her own bed, the tears nearly did what the river failed to do: *drown the brat*!

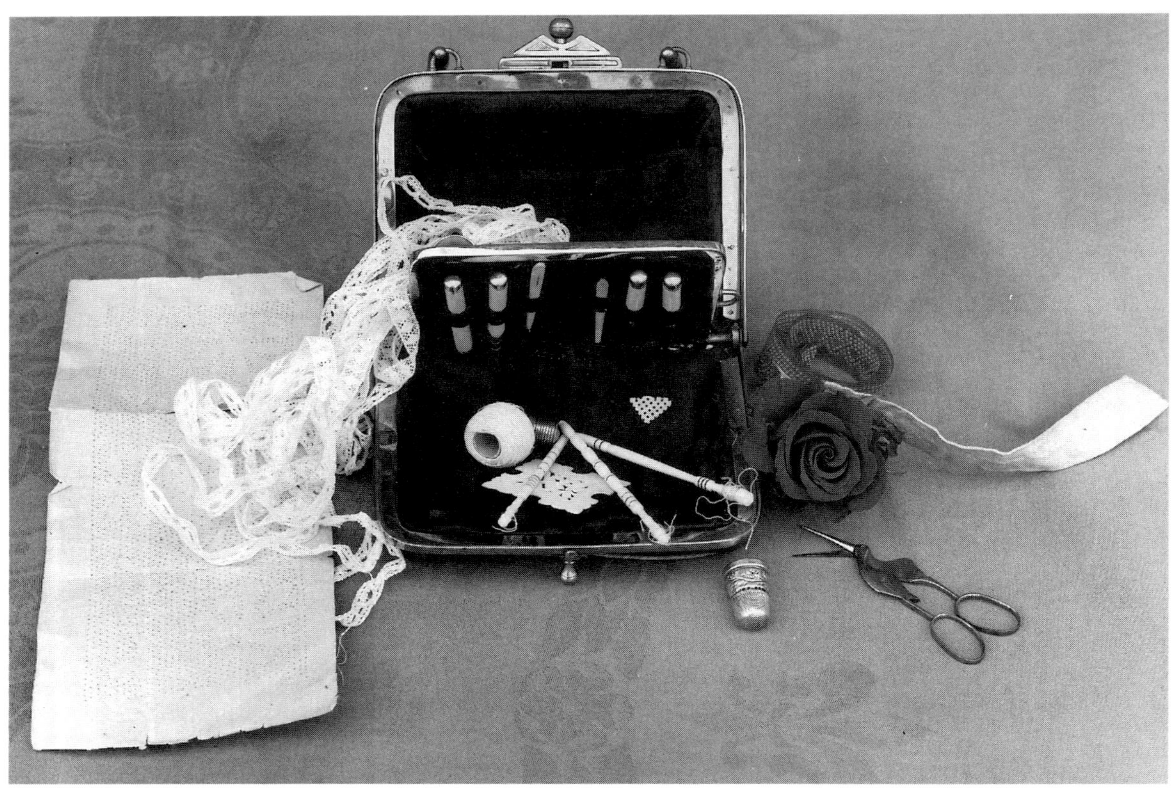

As the years went by, the three 'R's' under my belt, lace still the be-all and end-all in life, I progressed from chalk and blackboards to real writing books. School books in those days had embossed covers. Each new cover had the design 'lifted' off with a piece of paper laid over the top and then rubbed over with a pencil. With a 'bride' or a 'leg' or sometimes a mesh background laid in afterwards, there was always a design of sorts. I became very adept at leaving something out here and adding something in there, putting in a scroll or line to finish it off or to pull the whole thing together, just as Mother did.

It came to the notice of my teacher that there was perhaps a candidate for the Art College at a later date; but by the age of nine, not content with taking rubbings from the front of each book, bigger and better things arrived.

One particular arithmetic book had a super bobbin lace pricking on the front cover. Out came a page of squared paper, up went the lid of the desk and slowly, but very surely, the design was lifted off the cover and more slowly, but just as surely, the design was pricked out using school blotting paper underneath for a pricking board. What happened? I was caught, of course, taken down to the Headmistress's room, and given so many of 'the best' that I could not even close my hand, least of all write for the rest of the day. Left hands were specifically for the cane, right hands were for holding pens: that was another reason for not being left-handed in those days. Insult was added to injury when the Headmistress

sent a letter to Mother enclosing the sheet of paper that I had
'stolen' which had my lovely pricking on it. There was another
spanking and I was sent to bed with the pricking pinned to my
counterpane to remind me of my dreadful deed. That pricking is
now well over half a century old and getting very fragile like its
owner, but is still kept in a safe place amongst my souvenirs.

There was now a baby sister. I really did not remember her
coming. The baby just arrived one Saturday night. Maybe she was
one of those surprises that Father brought home for his family. I
thought the new arrival was lovely; all those gorgeous lace-edged
bonnets, silk coats covered in lace, and most of these clothes would

FIG 3.2 Chilprufe vests and pants
and Liberty bodices to keep out
the cold. Velour hats and kid
gaiters to keep head and legs
warm. The type of dress I was
expected to play in compared to
the clothes worn now. Believe it
or not, this is how I played on the
beach

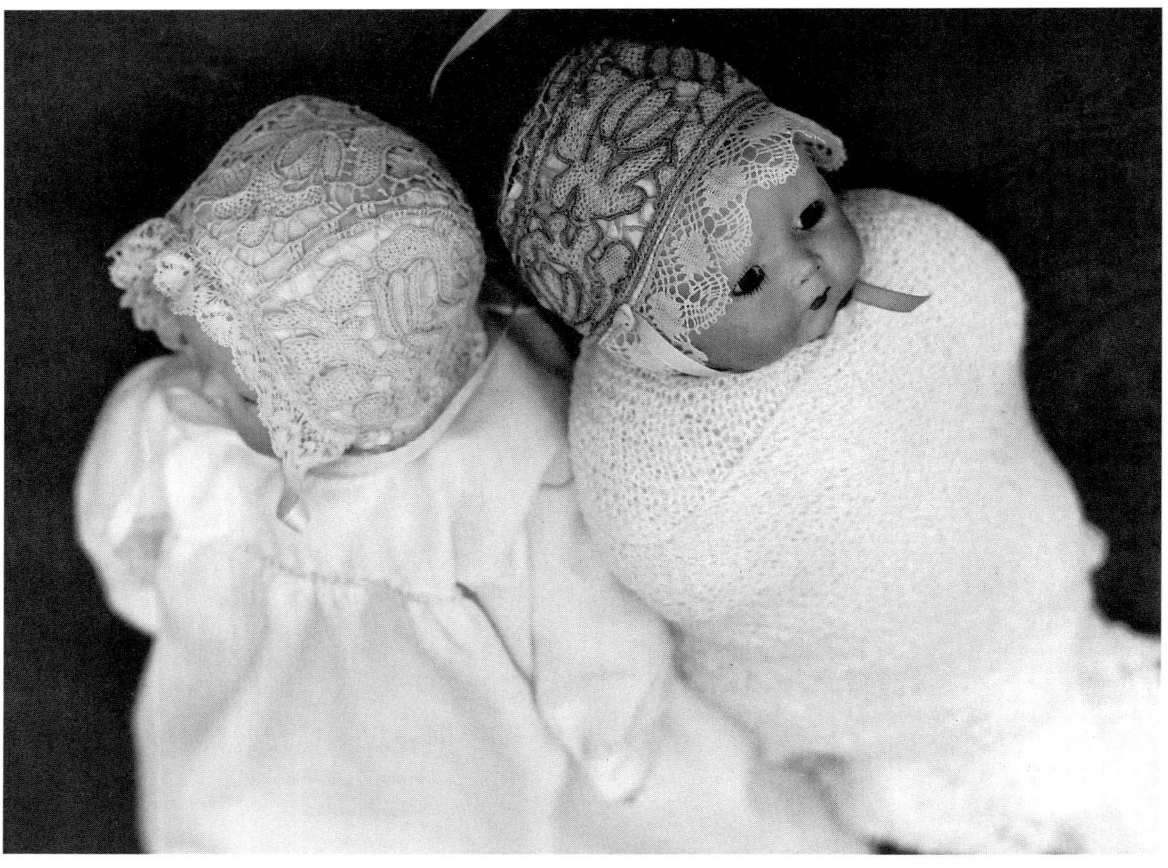

fit big doll. She in the cot grew, which was even better because her clothes really were passed on to big doll.

On Sundays (which started on Saturday evenings, when everybody would sit round the fire eating freshly-toasted muffins with lashings of butter), Mother would make her 'family' lace. It was maybe something for the home; other times it would be new cuffs and collars for herself; but, just sometimes, it would be for her daughters.

After Saturday tea would be the awful ritual of bath and hair-washing. Long ringlets grew to twice their length when wet, there were tears when the tangles were removed, then cuddles in front of the fire while it dried, then kisses and up to bed.

The bedroom had slatted wooden venetian blinds and by pulling the cords so that the slats sloped upwards, when the leaves of the trees blew in front of the gas lamps outside, patterns would ripple across the ceiling. When the tram passed by, the pattern would start half-way down one wall, travel up to the ceiling, bend in half, and chase across the ceiling before vanishing into the wall on the other side.

It was great fun making the moving lights into imaginary things. In the summer the sun would shine on the sea and send dappled reflections on to the ceiling. These did not disappear into the wall,

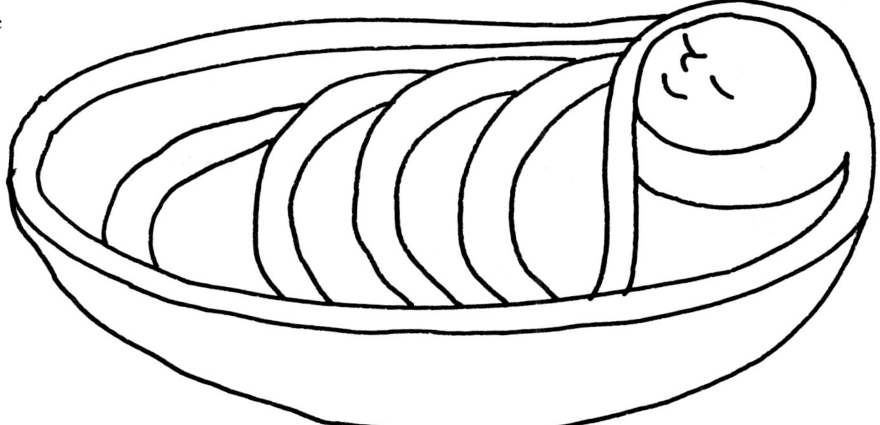

but remained as a thousand sparkling ripples or diamonds, or they could be golden buttercups blowing in a field, because these reflections could be all things to me.

Any spare time would find me lying on my tummy drawing the shapes that I could see on the walls and ceiling. I used to spend ages looking out of the window watching the shapes made by the sun as the waves rolled in. The white horses were lace collars – they were Venetian lace collars because the foam raised the edges and they looked like carvings.

A baby girl's bonnet

The original design for this bonnet was issued by the Butterick Publishing Co. in 1895, when it was suggested that it should be worked as Battenberg Lace. This is a tape lace with a number of different needlepoint lace stitches, using two or three different-sized threads. The tape used for the original design was a size No. 2, which was very narrow. The English Lace School now stock a very narrow tape which would suit this design.

For this book the design was reduced to fit a doll, so it is worked on a much smaller scale, too small to use even the narrowest tape available now. Therefore a cordonnet was laid using Gutermann 100/3s silk, the stitches were worked in Brillante D'Alsace 30 and the raising was done with the 100/3s.

The whole design was worked in the usual way and after the raising, it was removed from the background material and cleaned of all couching threads. Both side panels were then attached to the centre panel by closely buttonholding over the laid cordonnets of both the left hand side and centre panel, then working the right-hand side and centre panel in the same way.

There is a back and front to the centre panel; it is wider at the front and narrows down at the back to allow for shaping into the neck.

The scalloped edge was omitted because the scale was too small to take such a heavy finish. Instead make a little scallop of three laid threads, each worked over with eight buttonhole stitches worked at regular intervals of about 4 mm.

The lining of the bonnet is of fine silk. Cut four side panels and two centre panels, allowing for turnings. Make sure the back and front of the centre panels are correctly placed and the side panels are positioned correctly before making up. Make up the two separate bonnets, using small running stitches to join the panels together, and then place one inside the other with all the rough seams to the inside. Tack all round, turning the outside edges in as you work round the complete edge.

Carefully oversew the two pieces together, then work a row of either Spanish, Ardenza, or Alençon Point at regular intervals round the outside edge at the same distance as the edge stitches round the lace bonnet. Work as many buttonhole stitches as it takes to form a small scallop into each loop. Attach the ribbons to the silk bonnet to suit the baby's face. The lace bonnet is then laid over the silk one and tacked into place. Do not sew the two together permanently because the inner silk bonnet will need washing more often than the lace.

FIG 3.5 Bonnet design

FIG 3.6 (a) Kate Louise sitting at her lace, quite! content!! and fair of face counting her bobbins, one to nine – *nine?* three have gone astray. Emma has just passed this way; she's the culprit, does it every time; (b) Emma clambers off her seat: She has had plenty of practice at Beating the Retreat

In 1506 Stephen Grosson wrote.

> *Those aprons white of finest thread,*
> *So choicelie tide, so dearlie bought,*
> *So finelie fringed, so nicelie wrought.*
> *Were they in work to save their cotes*
> *They need not cost so many grotes.*

Aprons at the time of Queen Anne were very rich in needlework and often edged with gold lace and spangles. Many old paintings show ladies in all stations in life wearing them, so who are we to complain about wearing one? The difference is of course that ours has no gold lace or spangles. Even mine was a little different from the plastic one with the bib turned up at the end that catches anything that does not reach the mouth of the Tutankhamen sitting in the highchair.

> *Look well to what you take in hand*
> *for larning is better than any house or land,*
> *When land has gone and money spent,*
> *Then larning is most excellent.*

That was worked into a sampler by a Mary Saunders in 1717 when she was just nine years old.

On Sunday mornings I wore my 'best' clothes, made specially to wear on Sundays. It was a silly custom because children grew out of them then, just as they do now. There were very few shops that sold 'off-the-peg' clothes, apart from Liberty's or the Chilprufe range – at least, they were the only clothes which I can remember being sold in shops. Because Sunday clothes had to remain clean, aprons were worn during breakfast in case egg dribbled off spoons. Then faces were washed, hair carefully put into ringlets round Mother's finger and dropped into place. These were tied up with large ribbon bows, always white ribbon for Sundays. There were black ankle-strap shoes or white button-up boots. My Sunday dresses were always made from the left-overs from somebody's wedding dress or evening gown. Mind you, the material was always beautiful. Silks and poplins in summer, Pan Velvet with white lace collars in winter. What was lost on the roundabouts was gained on the swings, so the saying goes.

Sunday lunch was after Church. When Father had finished his glass of port he would sit in his chair. There was a suspicion that he slept, but nobody ever dared voice that opinion. He would sometimes tell stories until dinner at 6 o'clock and would then read his papers in the evening.

Something else confused me. Only when Father was home did dinner forget to come to the table at midday. There was another meal on Sundays that was called supper. Through the week it was called 'high tea', although it was always set on the same height table.

Did men ever work? That, too, puzzled me. Not a stroke through the week, not if all they did was working at being bored. I could be bored if I wanted to be. Grandma said boredom was having nothing to do. There was always work to do in her house. On Mondays, there would be Mrs Moss, who started the weekly wash 'before school' and would still be washing the floor when it was 'after school'. Grandma said she had her hands in water so long because she was so slow; that she gathered moss and that was why she had that name. She came again on Tuesdays and ironed piles and piles of the wash she had done the day before. By the time school was over she was sitting down goffering the pillow slips or pinning out the lace edges. I loved helping her to do that (Mrs M. thought I was an awful nuisance and was not backward in telling me so). Nevertheless, she spent ages over our Sunday dresses and Mother said it was because she did not have any little girls of her own.

By now there was a thing called a brother. He came wrapped up and when Mother washed him, he was dried and powdered then wrapped up again in lots of bandages all round his little tummy. Then on would go a nightdress and his hands would be tucked up in a fine wool shawl, so very tight that he reminded me of Tutankhamen's pictures I had been shown at school. The only reason for believing 'Boy' was alive and kicking was because he cried every time he was hungry. He certainly couldn't move anything else but his mouth. He had pretty little lace caps tied

60

under his chin with ribbon but it was ages before he had arms and legs. He always looked like a cricket bat tied up in a shawl but he improved and became a lovely blond, cuddly little boy. His sisters loved him for a while, then he managed to crawl and no toys were ever safe if left on the floor after that, so we both went 'off him'.

Tutankhamen's lace cap

This is based on the design given for the baby girl's bonnet. The same threads and tape can be used for the full-size version. Again the worked cap is for a doll and has been reduced in size. It is too small to use a tape. Gutermann 100/3s and Brillante D'Alsace has been used as was suggested on page 55.

There is a back and a front to the circle and the top of the main panel has two darts. Once the lace is worked the two darts are sewn up before attaching to the top. The scalloped edge is part of the design in this instance and it is advisable to measure the baby's head to make sure that the pattern is neither too big nor too small before working the lace.

Make up the two separate silk cap linings and sew them together; the directions given for putting the bonnet together can now be followed for the cap. The two darts should match up when putting the silk linings together; the centre back of the circle should line up with the join at the back of the main panel.

Back to this question about men never working. There was an awful lack of men in my childhood. 'Willie's girl' came on Wednesdays to clean brass, door steps and grates. Cooking was done in a big way on Thursdays by Mrs Moss. Grandma said it dried her out and got rid of the dry rot. On Fridays, 'Willie's girl' took the pony and trap to do the shopping, and also collected me from school.

This happened every five days between Sundays and Saturdays, when there was not a man in sight. 'Willie's girl' had a brother who did the garden after school, but he was only a few classes higher than me, so he wasn't really a man. Yet, come Saturday evening, Father was in his chair where he remained, except for Church and walks with the girls, until Monday. The only real work he did was to carve the meat and pour the wine. Mother could do both with less fuss and in half the time.

The only men that looked as if they worked were the shop-keepers, and they only took the money while the shopladies fetched and carried and tied the parcels up. Father and the man in Church read stories, but then so did Mother and Great Grand Mother. Great Grand Mother was better than any of them. If the Doctor came with his black bag, he sat by your bed and held your hand while he put his other hand on your head. Then, when he left, Mother found some money to pay for him coming. Mother and Grandma did the same thing and were more often right as to what was wrong with the child, and there was never anyone to pay them.

No, I was quite sure that women did all the work and that the man species disappeared for five days and only came back to be waited on at weekends. To be fair, I found out as I grew older that my Father was away working for the Cable and Wireless Company on the five fatherless days.

FIG 3.8 Cherry Ripe. A design to practise working bars and wheels

4

The lace fever

The lace fever, the symptoms and the cause

This is the tale of a parasol. When parasols came in for repair they were treated like gold dust. I was lucky if I saw them after they were mounted ready for their restoration. They would be kept wrapped in clean linen and only saw the light of day when somebody was working on them. Sometimes the old lace cover would be taken off, a new design made from it, and the old one thrown away. Once retrieved from the waste bin they made lovely veils when placed over a head of curly hair. Dolls would have their heads pushed through the hole in the middle where the ferrule went and a length of ribbon round dolly's middle made her the most elegant gown. This was a secret game, as neither Mother nor Grandma would allow a dirty piece of lace to be played with. One could never be sure whether 'She' carried an illness, 'She' being the owner of the old lace. So if one was caught playing with an old piece of lace it was always 'wash your hands and clean your nails'. Having washed my hands and cleaned my nails I could see no reason for not playing with the lace because there was no way in which I could then make it dirty.

Off to school one day, at the back of the house there was the bag left for the local dressmaker. All the 'tats' were kept for her, anything removed from dresses, hats, or whatever, left for the 'little woman' in a large pillowslip. No, the woman was not left in a pillowslip: the lace bits were. Right on the top was a beautiful parasol cover, black, extremely fine and just the loveliest design you ever saw.

The pony and trap was already out front, but out came the cover, a scramble up to my bedroom to conceal the lace under my pillow. No time to wash hands or clean nails, so it was a hurry back down to the waiting transport and away to school.

Back at home that afternoon there was an irate Mother waiting for her daughter. The girl who 'did', whatever that was, had found the parasol cover under my pillow when making the bed, and had reported the matter to 'Ma'am'. Ma'am had by now worked up quite a temper. Not only had the child done wrong in the first place, she had caused everyone unnecessary work. Sheets and pillowslips had required scrubbing, and today was not Monday. Mrs Moss was more than cross at having to get her hands all wet after drying out on Tuesday and when she had a full day ahead of her on Thursday. It meant my room had been disinfected with that awful smelling Lysol – it had all meant extra work. So to that awful-smelling room, without so much as a drink, I was sent to bed.

FIG 4.2 Angels squabbling? The best of siblings do. This design gives you the chance to use the grid lines

I lay there, tummy rumbling until it was nearly dark. I had drunk the water left for cleaning teeth, forgetting that it had salt in it (there was no toothpaste in those days), so I was desperate for a drink. Then the door opened, and there was Mother with a tray of bread and butter and a glass of milk.

Whilst kneeling by the bed, suffering those awful curls to be brushed, I heard Mother say 'I've never in all my life met anyone suffering so badly with the lace fever'. A kiss goodnight, tucked up in bed, and then 'worry'. What happened when you had lace fever? Was it very bad? Did you have to go into isolation, as you did with diptheria, or even die and go to heaven like they did in the isolation hospital? Would Mother bring up some of that dreadful Febrifuge, made from those vile-tasting flowers? Sleep came before the fever and in the morning I ate so much for breakfast I could not possibly be dying.

Anyway, if I had to die, it would have to be at school, because a lunch had been packed, the trap had arrived at the front and I was bundled into it. On arriving home I was summoned to Grandma's room and given a parcel. Someone had washed the parasol cover and there it lay in white tissue paper, clean, and all mine. What is more important, Grandma made a black butterfly from the thread that the new parasol cover was being worked with. From that day on I suffered with lace fever like a martyr, never complaining of my ill and always wondering in what form it would one day erupt.

There is one certain phenomenon about lace fever: the worse it

FIG 4.3 Siblings: who could be without them when bobbins become so tangled up? Nena Maria helping sister Olivia Fay come to terms with this two-over-three bit

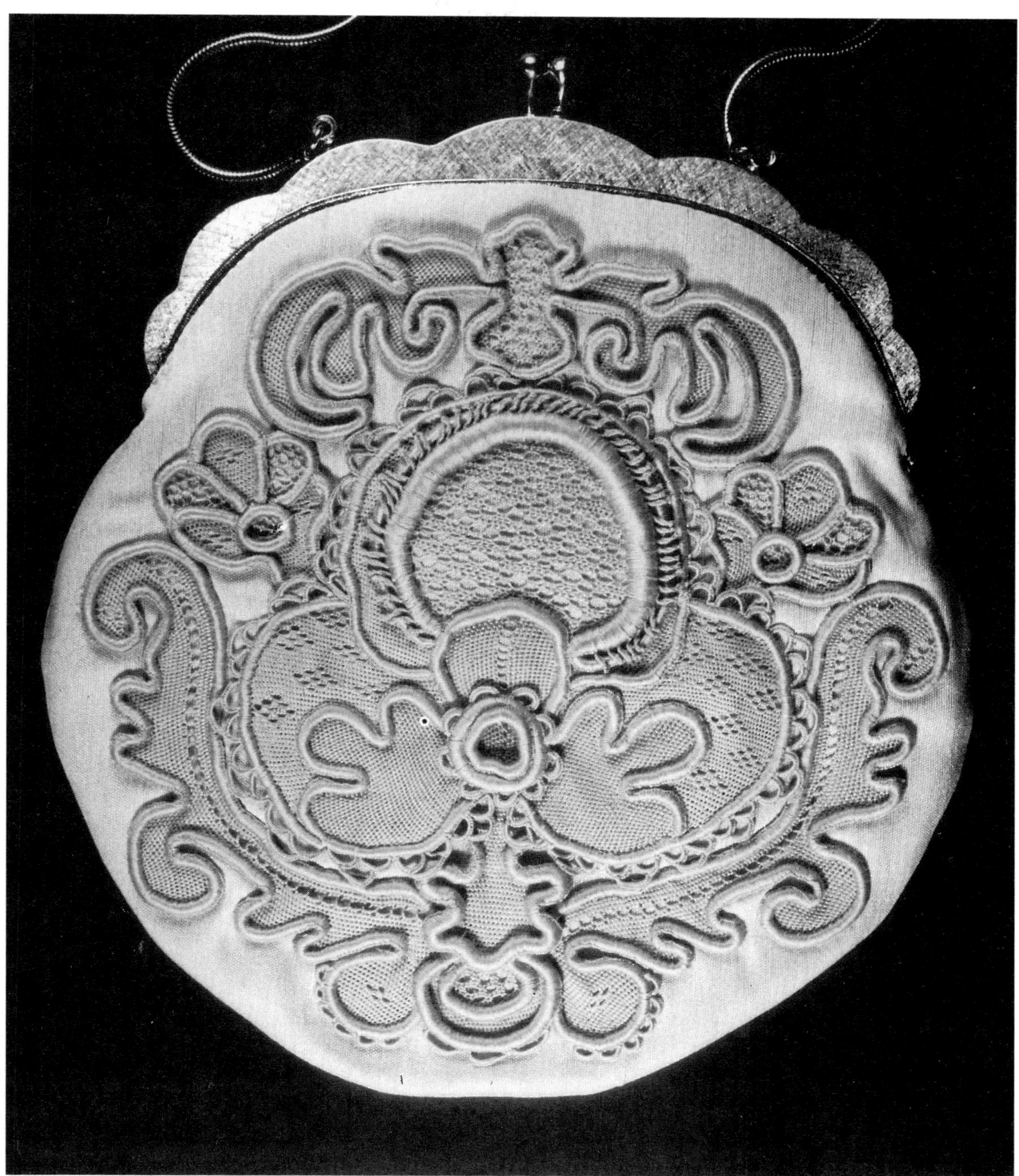

FIG 4.4 Although this beautiful piece of work by Catherine Barley is certainly not a work bag, I'm sure it will heighten all her charms when she allows it to dangle from her arm. Another of her bags is on the front jacket of *Introduction to Needlepoint Lace*

At the end of the 1790s handbags were known as '*ridicules*' or '*indispensibles*'; before that, they were called '*knotting bags*'.

Meanwhile to heighten all her charms
the workbag dangled on her arm;
The very bag that British Belles
Bear on their arms at Tunbridge Wells

from *The London Magazine or Gentleman's Intelligencer* (1764).

becomes, the more you enjoy it. In most cases it is fatal, and there is no cure. It is like 'flu, in as much as there are a variety of different types of bug that can hit you. Reading the many books available on the subject only makes things worse, because they seem to suggest that you have more symptoms than you first thought, which in turn gives you more enjoyment.

When starting out on the first flush of a high temperature, sit quietly and reflect for a while on the most likely cause. Is it bobbins and pillows? A stab from a needle from needlepoint lace? Or is it collecting for the sheer pleasure of handling the lace? Whichever the cause, once started off on the road to the City and Guild Examination in Lace, you will all be suffering from it.

To help you make your own diagnosis, here are some distinctive characterisations of the symptoms.

Punto Tagliato à Fogliami. Punto = Stitch, and *Tag* = cut. The *fogliami* is the design. This was the forerunner of *Punto in Aria*, which means stitches in the air. The use of the *Cordonnet* first appeared in *Venetian Point*, and was soon practised by most of the lace workers of Europe.

Then followed *Punto Roselline* or *Rose Point*. It was given this name because of the tiny roses worked into every available space in the design. Soon the workers were superimposing roses on roses and even placing them on the bars as well as on the actual design. Whole edges were composed of tiny roses in miniature pots. The variety known as *Point de Neige* was very much like Rose Point but had tiny stars worked in the same manner as the roses in the previous lace. *Point de Venise à Reseau*, a needlelace of the greatest delicacy, followed. In case the name should cause you anguish at a later date, try to remember *Punto Avoria*, which was a beautiful lace made in *Valle Vogna* in Northern Italy. This combined bands of silk or linen with lacework.

When Colbert encouraged the Italian lace workers to settle in France during the reign of Louis XIV, the French industry took the lead on the continent. Italian laces were no longer imported into France. It was all *Point de France*, *Point d'Alençon* and *Point d'Argantella*. A good guide to the last-named is the use of *Partridge Eye* ground, the numerous fine *Jours*, and what was known as the *Mayflower Pattern*. Flanders was known for its wonderfully fine thread as much as for the lace it produced. Among these laces were *Bruxelles Point* and later *Point de Gaze*, all of which were of gossamer fineness. Into the nineteenth century there were the laces of *Brabant*, *Mechlin*, *Antwerp*, *Valenciennes*, *Binche*, and so was established *Trolle Kant* or *Fil Conenu*, a net made with bobbins on a pillow. *Vrais Reseau*, or *Droschel*, indicates that it is a hand-made bobbin net. The lace was worked in long narrow strips which were joined together with the *Point de Raccroche* stitch.

There is a lot of confusion over *Point d'Angleterre*. The name was in common use through the seventeenth century but whether it was worked by Flemish workers who migrated to England or was worked by English lacemakers before that, is debatable, so try not to get drawn into that argument.

One thing is certain: there were two grounds that distinguished Brussels lace. The earliest was the *Bride*, which was very expensive to make as it was time-consuming. The other was the *Reseau*. Both were hand-made. If it was made with a needle it was called *A'Largelle*, if made with bobbins it was *Au Fuseau*.

The workers were highly specialised and had various titles to denote the type of work they did. The young girl starting her apprenticeship was called the *Ecole Dentellier*, and, at a very early age she earned enough from her lace to maintain herself and often an ageing parent. There was the *Dentellier* who worked the footings, the *Fonneuse* did the openwork, while the *Droscheleuse* made the *Vrai Reseau*, and the *Jointeuse* assembled it all. There are other titles and some are listed in *The Techniques of Needlepoint Lace*. *Point De Malines* is a bobbin lace, although *point* means needle and as a rule anything with the word *point* in it indicates that it is a needle-made lace – but there are exceptions to every rule. *Mechlin Lace* was said to have been Napoleon's favourite lace. In the early Mechlin Laces there are a number of different grounds, but a popular one with the workers seems to have been *Fond de Neige*. Do not get this mixed with the *Point de Neige*, which is a needle-made lace. A design attributed to Antwerp was *Potten Kant*, in which the flower-pot was symbolic of the Annunciation. *Ghent Lace* flourished in the Beguines, which was a religious sisterhood, but it was the making of the machine net and lace that put Ghent firmly on the lace map.

Holland was known for its gold and silver lace, introduced by a man called Simon Chatelain. *Lille Lace* is much like *Mechlin*. Black silk lace was produced at Lille for a short time in the eighteenth

FIG 4.6 The following pieces are
from the Ann Aldridge
collection: (1) Honiton lace; (2)
A length of Youghal; (3) This is
the head section of a pair of very
long lappets. Brussels needlelace,
second half nineteenth century;
(4) One of a pair of cuffs, Point de
Gaze; (5) An Irish crochet lace
parasol in cream with a black
fringe. It has a carved folding
handle; (6) Point de Gaze
flounce, about 3 metres long

FIG 4.7 Point de Gaze handkerchiefs from the Ann Aldridge collection

FIG 4.8 The following two pieces
are reputed to have been cut from
a Russian wedding veil. The crest
is actual size. From the Ann Aldridge
collection

century. *Le Puy* produced masses of lace in the seventeenth century, copied from the *Lille Lace* in design. Lace was made at Arras from very early dates in lace history. The *Mignonette* pattern distinguished it and is that for which it would be remembered. *Gold lace* was also produced here.

Blonde Lace was so called because at one time it was made from Chinese floss silk. It can be in its natural colour but a lot of it was dyed black. The dye was not very good and after a while it turned an awful shade of grey/green. It also rotted it over the years.

The popular *Black Blonde* was used for mantillas. Designs were of Spanish origin and changed very little even though it was made well into the twentieth century. *Spanish lace* is another that has doubtful origins. Some historians say that needlepoint was learnt from Italy and it was very much of the *Venetian Point* influence. Other authorities say it was the lace workers of Flanders, which was a Spanish dependency, who taught the art of pillow lace. Maybe both versions are right. Needlepoint lace was definitely made in Spain and would have come from Venice, while the later pillow lace could also have come from Flanders. That is what is called diplomacy, and when making this sort of statement it is

FIG 4.9 A corner from the Point de Gaze handkerchief, belonging to Ann Aldridge

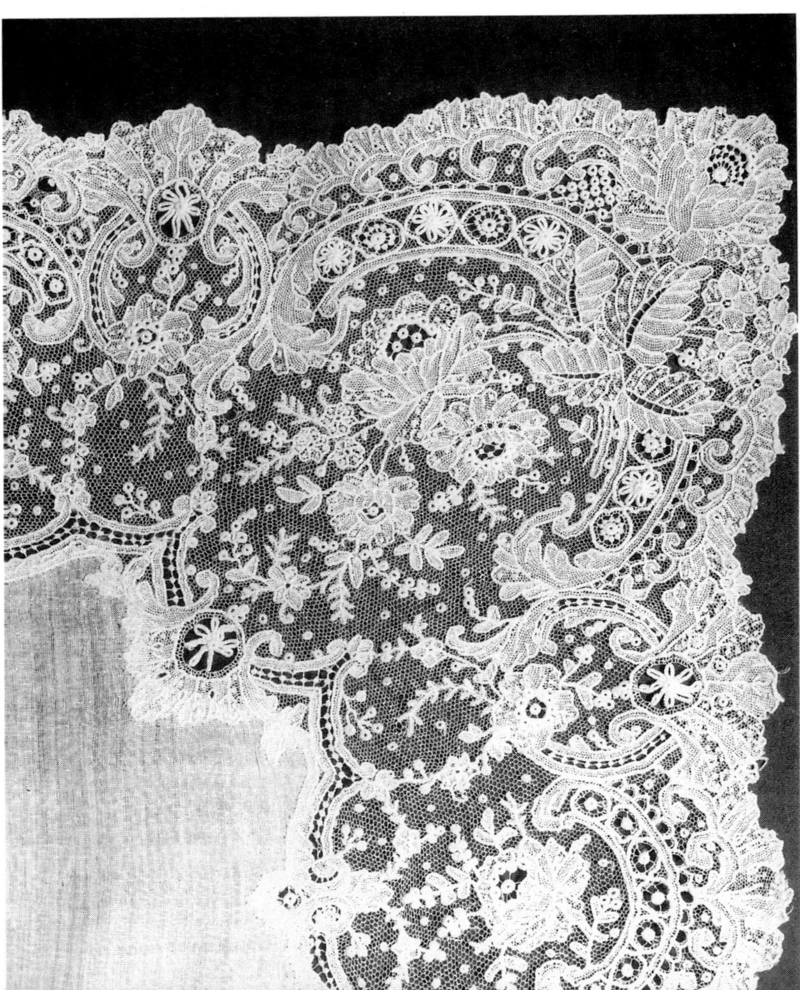

FIG 4.10 Blonde lace. This design
could be 'lifted' and used for
many different types of lace

FIG 4.11 My Mother's wedding
handkerchief, made for her by
her Mother

FIG 4.12 Nightdress top worked on double net in Tambour and needlerun stitches. The drawback stitch allows the net to be cut tight up against the stitches. Always wash the net before starting to work on it, in case of shrinking

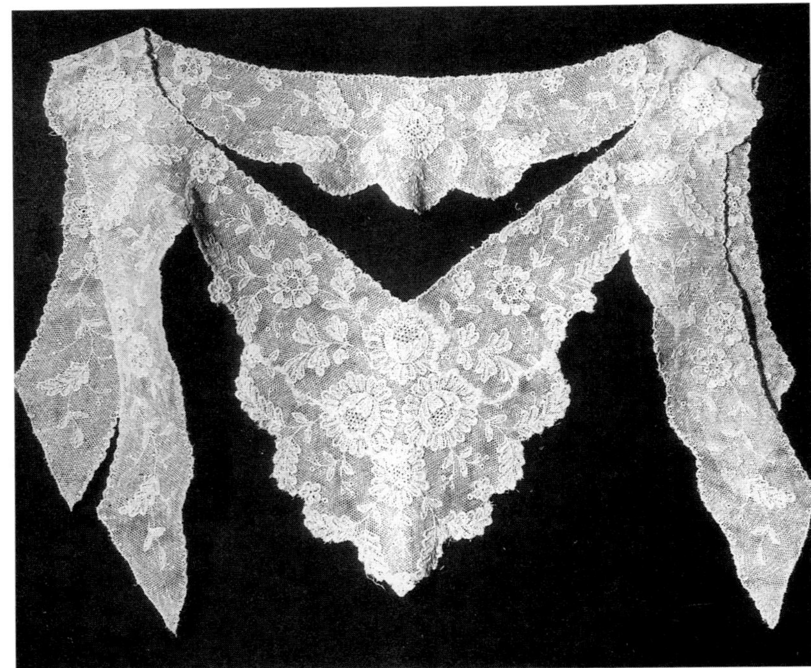

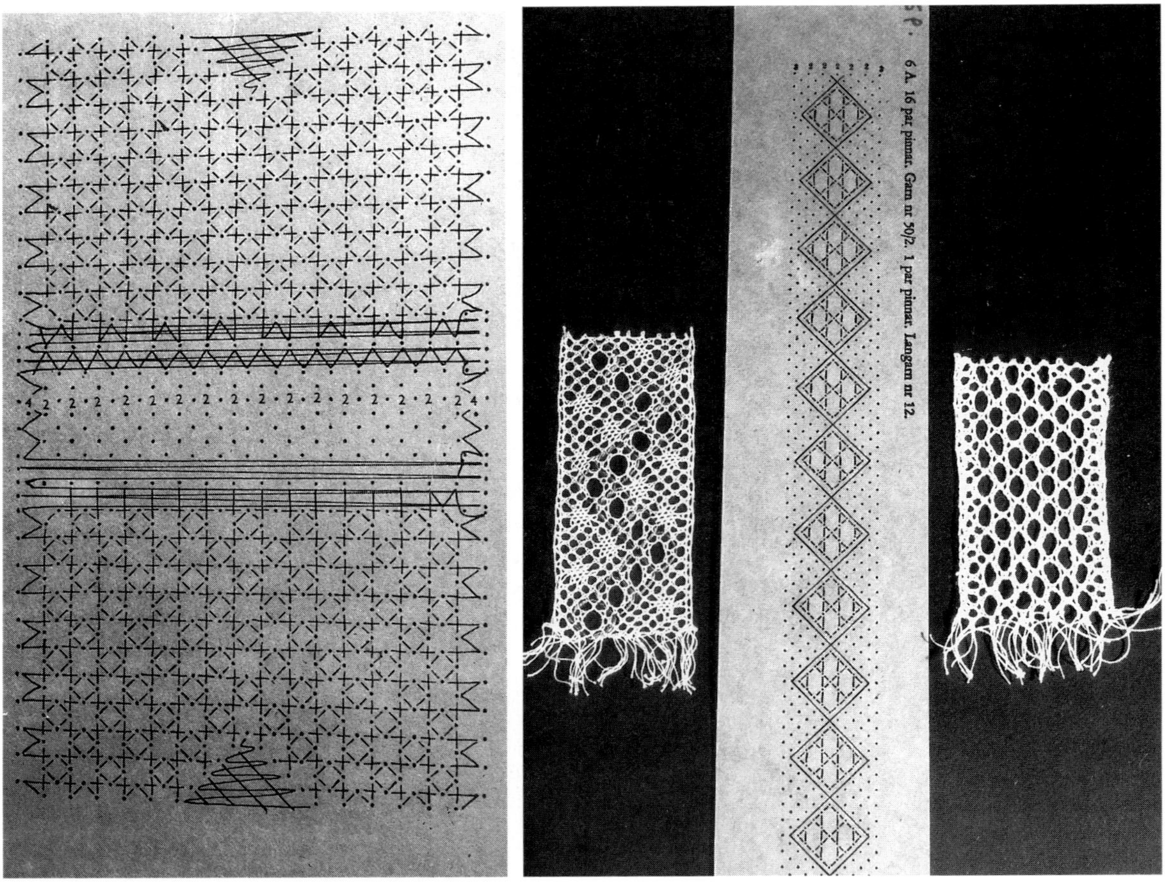

FIG 4.13 Virgin ground and the Rose ground prickings, which have two little sample pieces that were worked by Babs Ingledew

something you have to be well aware of. Someone will always prove you wrong. *Sans Sols* is of Spanish origin and was taken to *Teneriffe* to become known better there than in its original home. *Maltese Lace* is usually worked in silk and always has the Maltese Cross worked into the pattern so it is very easy to identify. *Point de Turque* is from Morocco and is worked completely in Rhodi or Smyna knots. There is a photo of a mat made of this lace worked by my mother in *The Technique of Needlepoint Lace.*

Tonder Lace is a bobbin-made lace from Denmark and the town of Westtena was the centre of lace in Sweden. There was a lace factory at Novgorod, in Russia, and there are pieces of lace that actually came from there in 1893, brought home by my Grandfather, now amongst my lace collection.

Torchon means duster, which is very cruel, because when worked with fine thread on a small scale it can look lovely. Before we go any further there is a lost stitch in Torchon lace, called Rose Ground. Now I hear a lot of you say, but we do work 'Rose Ground'. But no, most of you do not. What you are working is usually *Maidens Ground, Point de Marriage* or *Virgin Ground.* The pricking for Rose Ground is just like *Honeycombe* stitch of *Bucks Point* except that it is worked on a 45 degree angle. It is very pretty and the two prickings show the difference in the way the two stitches are worked. There was a certain Author who changed the name back in the 1930s, and everyone since has copied her. The one exception is Virginia Churchill Bath; the stitches are right in her book *Lace. Thre: de Dillmont* shows both stitches very clearly in her book. The book was published in English to coincide with the first Daily Mail Lace Exhibition held at the Royal Horticultural Hall, Vincent Square, Westminster, in 1908, and was sold for the grand sum of 1/3d (before decimal currency). Now a good secondhand copy would cost around £13. It's the greatest *little* book there ever was.

DMC Torchon Prickings are correctly named as are the *Knypling* prickings. Any of the pre-1914 books is right. There must be standardisation of stitch names if the City and Guilds examination assessors are not to be sent crazy trying to decipher which stitch is which name. England was more famous for *Opus Anglicanium,* which was an embroidery known across the Continent. Lace came to these shores via the refugees fleeing from one Edict or another over the years, and as they settled in certain parts of the country, so their particular type of lace took the name of the county that it was made in. There are four distinct bobbin laces, Bucks Point, Northamptonshire, Bedfordshire and Devonshire (which is normally called *Honiton Lace*).

Branscombe Point is another Devonshire lace that is made with a bobbin tape outline, and needlepoint fillings. Today it is usual to use machine-made tape. Do you remember how to tell the difference? Remember those far off days at the Tebbs School and my first lace. If, after all this, your mind is still functioning and you haven't stars in your eyes, then there is every likelihood that you will sit that exam and of course you will receive distinctions. Right at the beginning of this book you were told to think *high rise.*

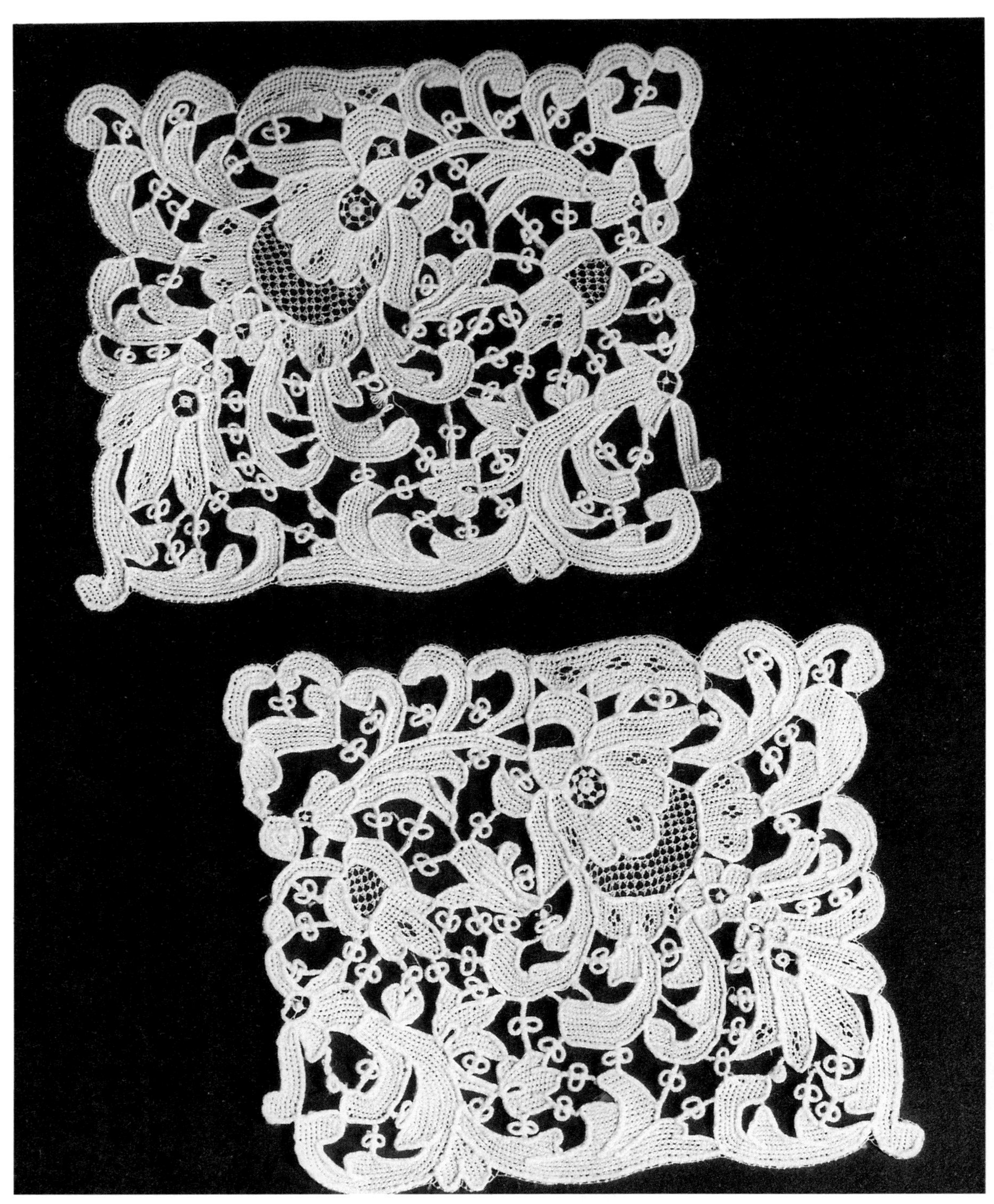

FIG 4.14 Two pieces of Burano
lace. The design has been
adapted by my son Neil to make
the Guild of Needle Laces
Trophy

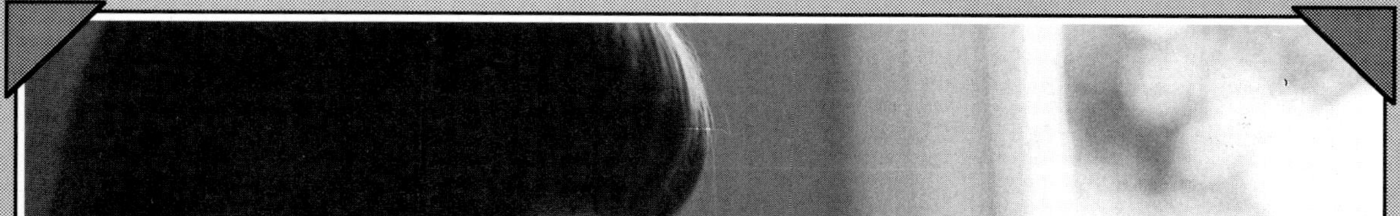

FIG 4.15
Pippa Louise lives in Parkstone Poole,
not a stone's throw away from Kemp Welch School.
So she is determined to become extremely good
and so join the lace makers of the neighbourhood.

When I was a child, Sundays were special. They really started at
tea-time on Saturday – four o'clock, that is. For one thing Father
would be there. It often went through my brain that Father
materialised on Saturdays, managed to stay visible all through
Sundays, then disappeared for the next five days. There were two
or three reasons why he just had to be around but could not be
seen.

For instance, Father had the biggest and best chair. It was
covered in red velvet and had antimacassars on the arms and over
the back. Now, if a child should sit on that chair during the five
fatherless days, it would be told, 'Please remove your bottom from
your Father's chair'. Why?

Beside the chair there was a round table that had drawers
underneath which held dominoes and chess pieces. If a school bag
or books were accidentally laid on it there would be 'take that off
your father's table at once'. That was why I often wondered if
Father was sitting there all the time but was invisible, because it
was neither Saturday nor Sunday. In the end, I never sat there in
case he was. The table had a round lace mat on it that remained the
same design whichever way round it was turned. It was a clever
design because it was just three of the same that made a ring.

I would sit on the floor and try very hard to see how three 'units'
could be designed to fit a ring so perfectly. Suppose one unit had
not been that exact shape? How did one get each unit so correct?
What if the ring had been bigger and the units could not have
reached each other – what would have happened to the gap that
would have appeared somewhere in the ring?

It was Grandma who answered all these questions, and made it
all look so easy. Now you can have the secret of designing for
circles, without maths or calculators. It's fun and the finished
drawing looks quite professional. The basic unit that we will use as
a repeat is very much like the one on the table that belonged to my
father.

Grandma used an HB pencil, which was not too soft, tracing
paper, cow-gum and oilskin. You will use an HB pencil, tracing
paper, Sellotape and draughtsman's linen. Decide what you want
to use your mat for; this decides the size it will be. You can then
play with the design, either enlarging it or reducing it to fit.
Remember the word 'Scale'?

This first time make it fit a place-mat; you might even go on to
make enough mats for a full setting for six!

The best template to use for this is a dinner plate. Turn it upside
down on the tracing paper and draw round it. The plate should be
laid tight up to one corner so that it touches the edge on two sides of
the paper. You will thus waste only the corner but you will have
enough paper to draw the design on. With the plate in the correct
position draw right round it. From now on take each step slowly
and you will not go wrong.

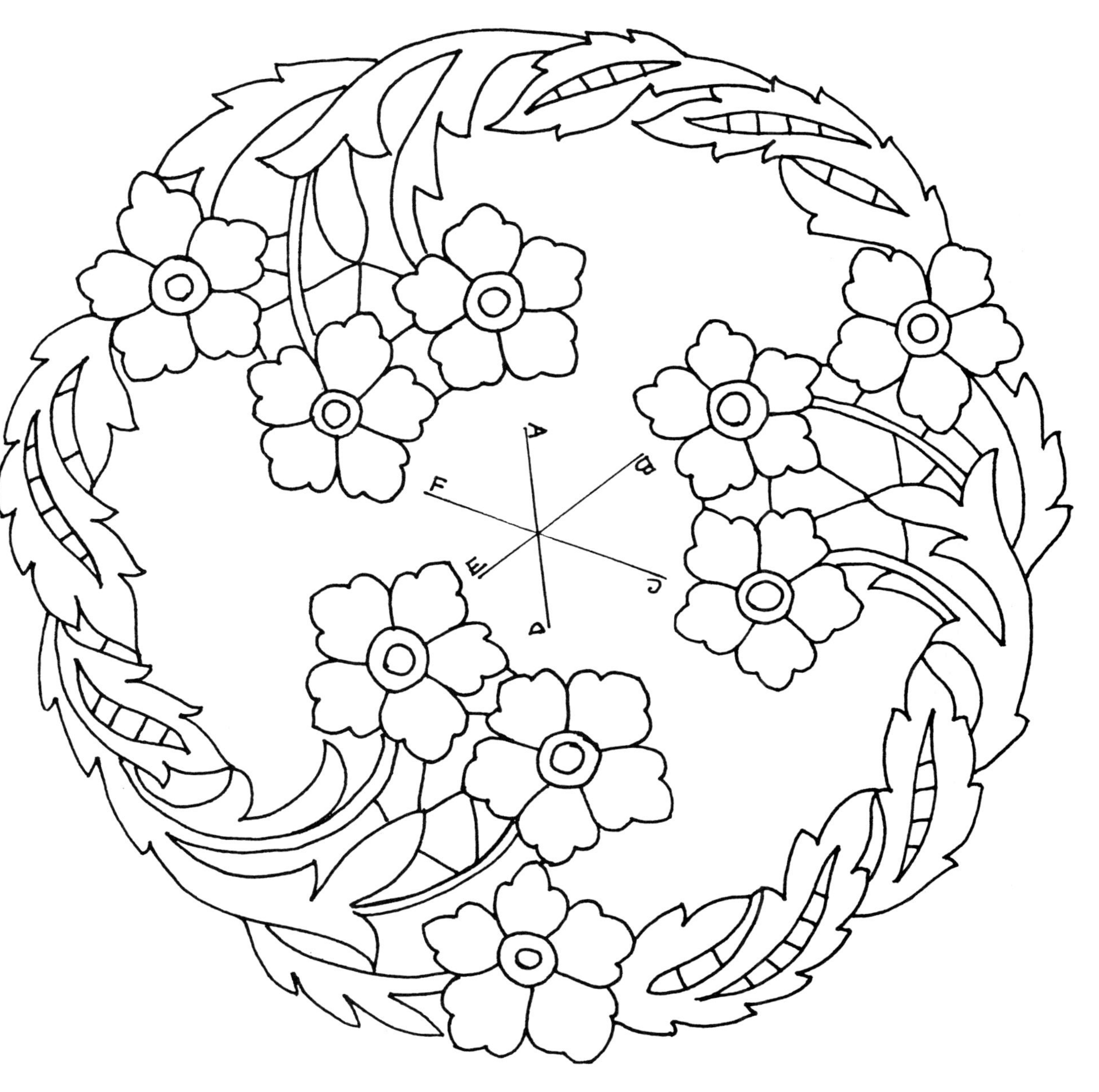

FIG 4.16 Three of a kind that made a ring

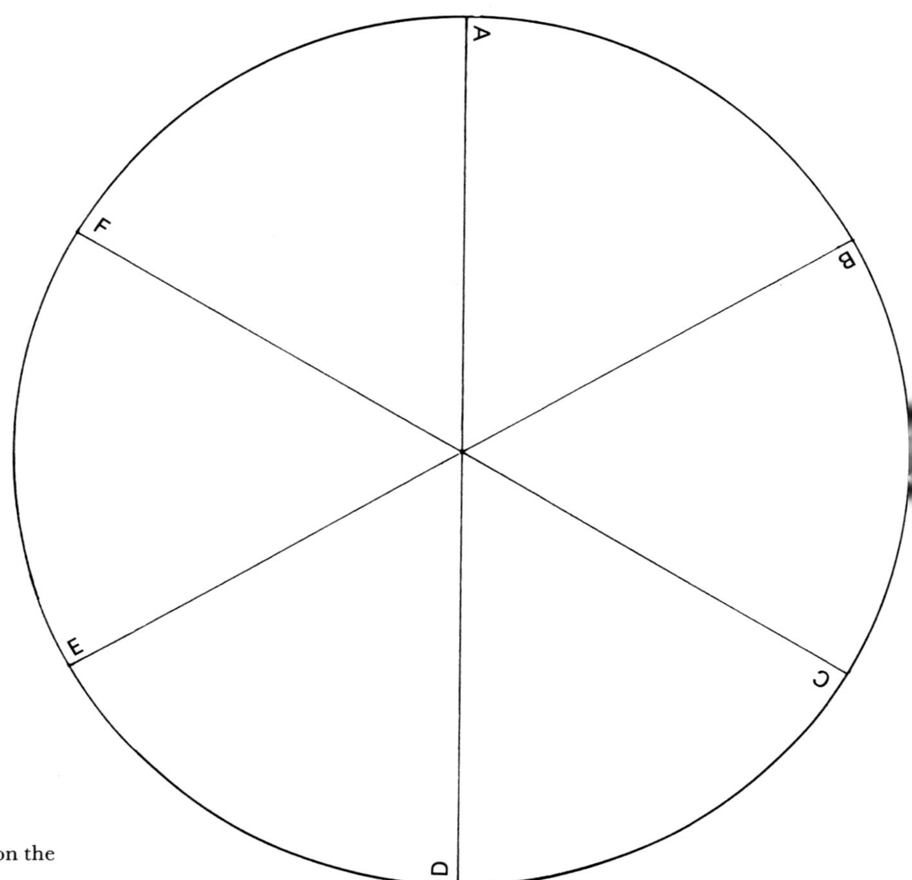

FIG 4.17 Placing the letters on the
folds

Three of the same, that make a ring

1. First cut out the circle you have drawn round the plate.
2. Fold the circle in half.
3. Divide the half circle into three equal sections and crease into wedges, then open out into a full circle again.
4. Pencil through the centre crease from one side to the other and mark the two points A and D. Turn the circle round to the next crease, pencil across and mark the points B and E. Then round to the next crease, pencil through it and mark the last two points C and F.
5. Fold across the centre line, A to D.
6. Hold at points C and E and open the two sides, B and F.
7. Bring up the point A to meet C-E, between B-F which will turn the paper into a three-point dart.
8. Run your fingers down the folds from B, F and D down to the bottom of the dart.
9. Bring point F and lay edge to edge at D. This gives a wedge with a slightly curved top.
   So far – so good. Now to make a design to fit your circle.

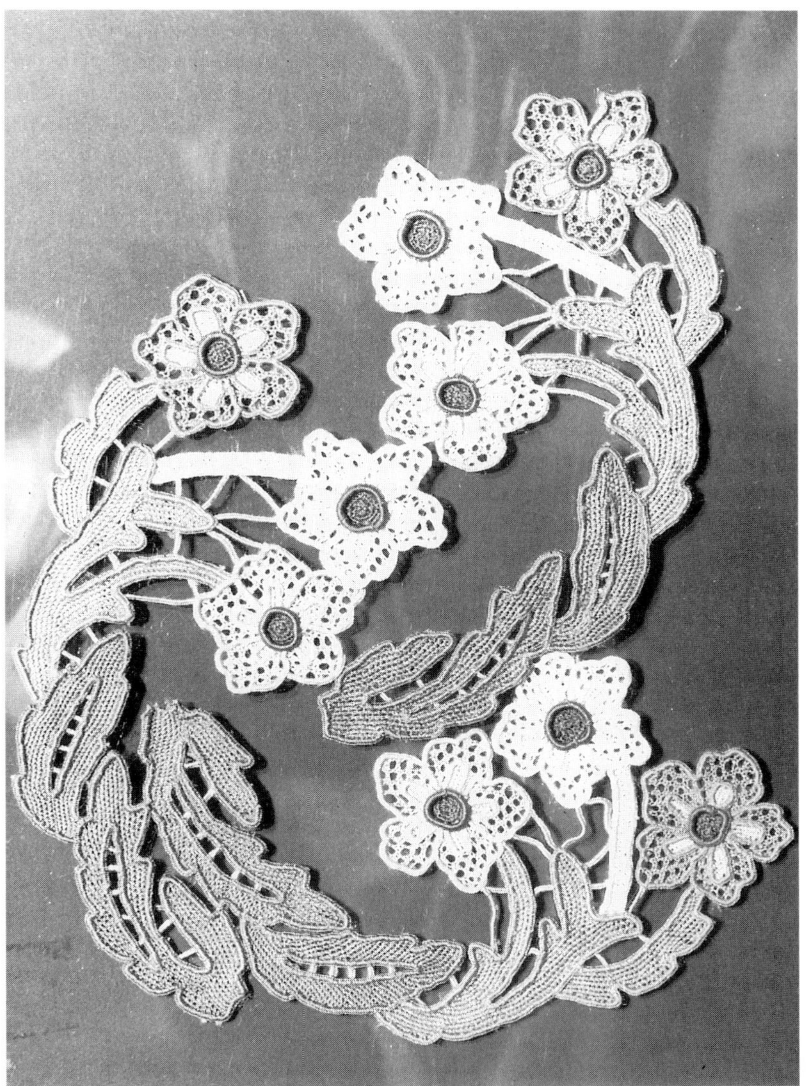

Trace off the units on page 81, and cut them into separate
sections. We have a slight problem now, because nobody knows
what size each of you has chosen. There is no such thing as a
standard-size plate.

The basic shape can be reduced to just the three flowers and
their stalks, and even further by using one of the pair as an
individual unit. Make use of the leaves, to sweep round the circle
where needed.

Place the design along the top curve of the wedge from point
B to D. Keep the cut-out paper in position with Sellotape.

Take a piece of the remaining tracing paper, lay it over your
design and trace it off.

Make two more tracings.

Lay the circle out flat and your traced designs should lie around
the edge of your circle, from B to D, from B to F, and from D to F.

Suppose at this point the design is not quite as you had intended it to be – you are not really happy with it. This is where the designer in you takes over. You will slightly turn the cut shapes into a curve or '*interlace*' the stalks, maybe lay one leaf over another, maybe add an extra leaf; each of you will make an individual design which will make the finished article your own.

The previous information is on the assumption that your plate was smaller than the finished design, so let us now increase the basic design.

If you took your drawing right up to the very edge of the wedge at the top when you laid the first unit, there could be very small gaps (or even very large gaps) at each fold. There are two ways to overcome this. All the design can be moved slightly toward the centre. It could be that only a fraction will be enough to join up the units, but this will still reduce the size of the finished mat. If you want to keep the original size, the leaves can be lengthened at the end of each stalk, or you can even add an extra leaf at the end of each unit. Another way would be to rearrange the position of the units and have them lying along the edge of the circle instead of curling up towards the centre of the mat as in the original.

The half flower, at the end of the first leaf of each unit, is the further two petals at the end of the complete unit. To keep the design running true this should join up, while other areas of the design are elongated.

You should now have a design something like the one I referred to as 'just three of the same that made a ring'. As we progress through this book there will be other designs to put together along the same lines as this one. The reason that you are using a set design, which is perfectly laid out to form a ring in the first place,

FIG 4.19 The one motif. If not being used as a ring the top two petals should be left out

and then encouraged to vandalise it and rearrange it, is for two reasons. First, it just goes to show how easy it is to create something that is all your own, by taking parts of a design and turning them into something individual. Second, it has made you look at a design and see it, not as a whole, but as pieces of a unit.

Designing is actually seeing things in an abstract way: seeing something and taking it out of context, to be used in a completely different way. For example, next time you pass a pair of wrought iron gates, stop and look at the design. Normally there will be scrolls, the same scrolls that you might easily find in the next piece of lace you look at.

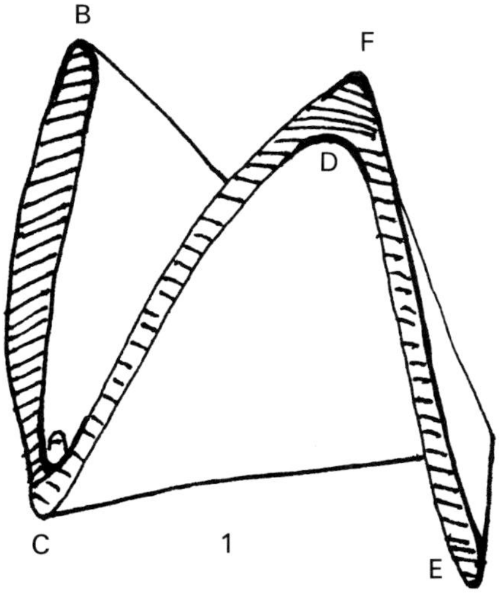

FIG 4.20 (1) The paper pattern folded; (2) A single unit that might be needed to enlarge a design; (3) Reducing the unit to make smaller circles

If and when you start to teach, remember this little tip. Never mention the removal of the couching stitches. Remember the first lot you had to remove and keep your lips firmly closed. Let that be another lesson for the future

An early lesson to learn is to never expect to work a piece of lace in a hurry. Let it remain a pleasure to do, not a chore that has to be done. There are days when you don't feel particularly interested in working it, and the needle picks up the 'vibes' and takes on a will of its own. You have no idea how many mistakes the needle can make if you are not on the same wavelength. So put the lace away, and do something else for a while.

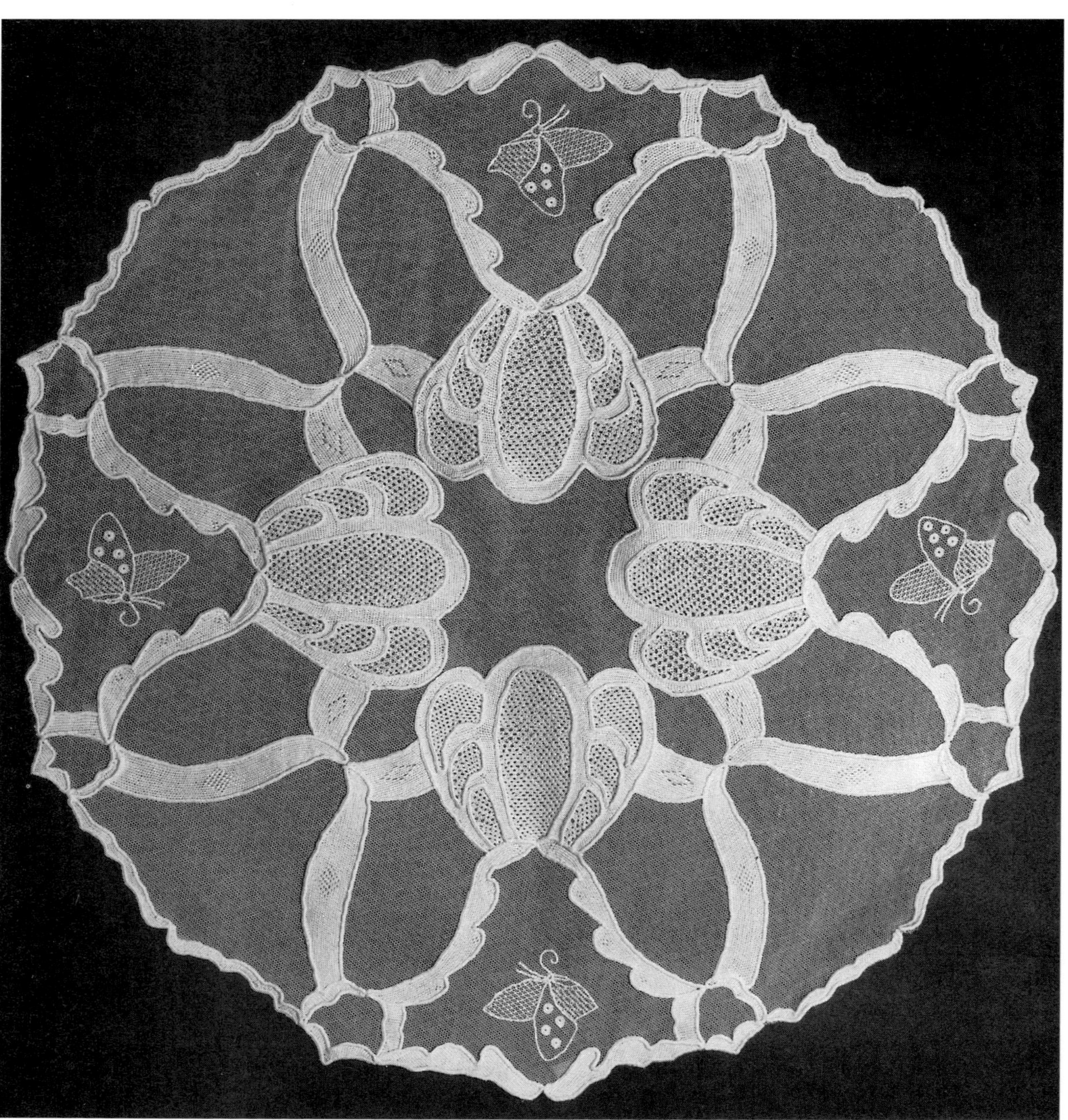

FIG 4.21 Round table mat. 76 cm diameter, worked in 100/3s Gütermann silk. Designed by the Author using the ring technique and worked by Winnie Hunt

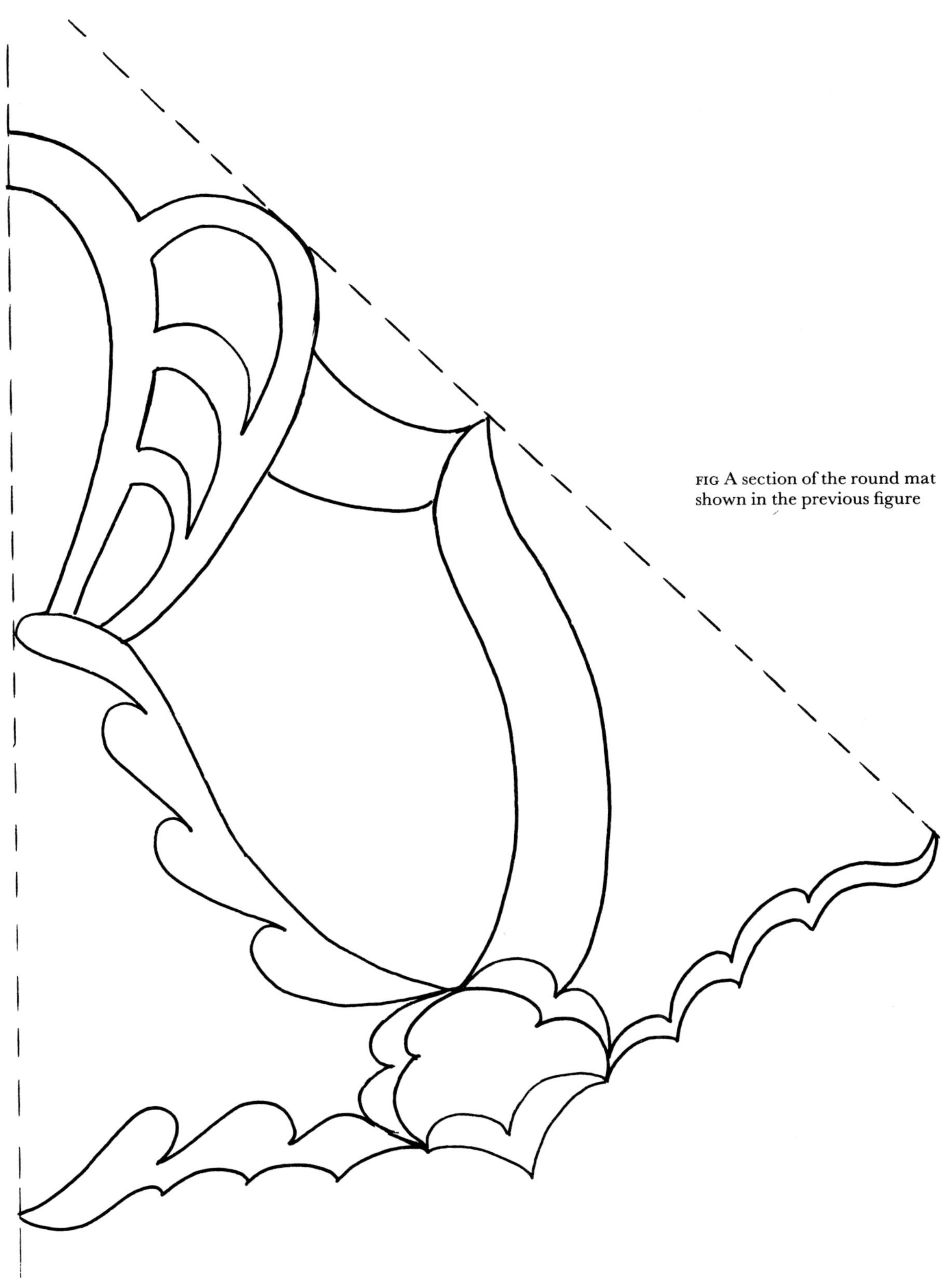

FIG A section of the round mat shown in the previous figure

FIG 4.23 The mirror image of the
previous section

FIG 4.24 One grand-daughter
thought this was a drawing of two
frogs, but it was not intended to
be. Four pairs will make a ring

FIG 4.25 The single motif turned
in the opposite direction, which
makes the top of the design
become the outline

FIG 4.26 Everyone who has seen this book in the making has asked for an enlargement of this design. It has been suggested that it could be worked in 80 crochet cotton as a repeat for the edge of a roller blind. Work on the ring principle for the edge of a round tablecloth in the same thread. Worked in finer threads it has endless possibilities

FIG 4.27 Another design based on
the folded circle using five
asymmetric motifs, repeated, not
mirror-imaged

In this book there will be no detailed instructions for the various lace stitches, as they have been given in the other books. Just to refresh your memories of the more intricate ones here are a few photographs that are easy to follow.

Having said that, I should add that this book was intended as 'A Letter To My Granddaughters'. In fact, the first draft went to the Publishers under that title. One of the eight-year-olds was asked to 'read' these photographs, and the instructions given are as she recorded them. It makes sense to her and to the older children, so it must make sense to adults now the letter has gone public.

Photograph No 1 (FIG 4.28)

Foundation Row Make a stitch, leave a space of 1, make a stitch then leave a space of 3, continue across the row

1st row 1 into first loop, 3 into the next. Repeat to the end of row

2nd row 1 before and after the single stitch, leaving space of 3. Repeat across the row

3rd row 3 between the pairs of stitches, 1 in loop under the 3 of the previous row. Repeat to end

4th row Repeat the 2nd row

Photograph No 2 (FIG 4.29)

Foundation row of evenly spaced stitches

1st row 1 into first loop, miss 2 loops, 1 into next loop, work to the end of row

2nd row Work 5 stitches into each long loop

3rd row Work a stitch each side of the centre stitch of the 5 above, and 2 into each loop between the blocks of 5

4th row Work 2 before the pair of the centre stitches of the block of 5 of the previous row, 1 between the centre stitches and 2 into the next loop. This brings you back to the blocks of 5

6th row starts the pattern again at 2nd row

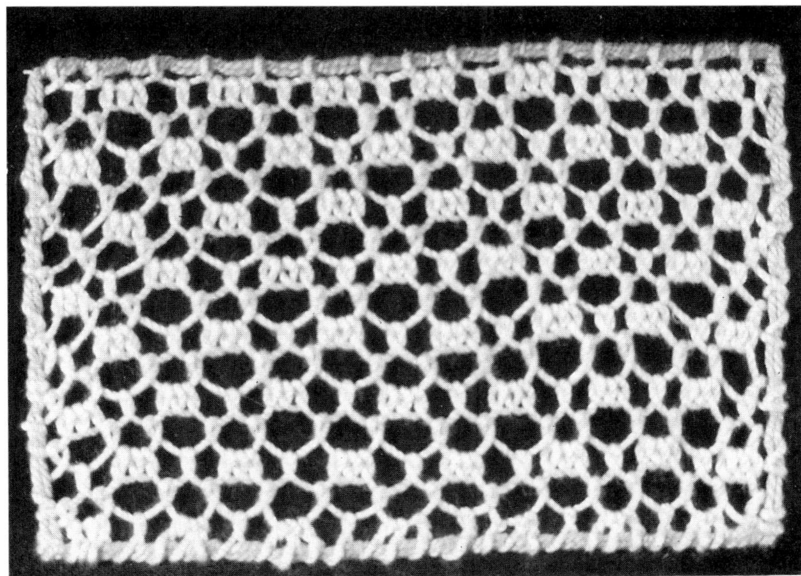

FIG 4.28 Pea Stitch variation (see page 37 *Introduction to Needlepoint Lace*)

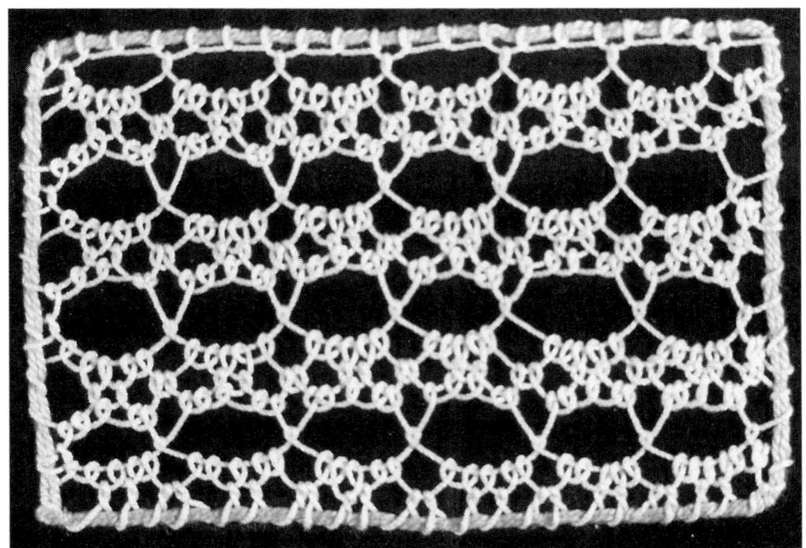

FIG 4.29 Ground from Paraguay. Shown on page 90 of *Creative Design in Needlepoint Lace* in the sampler worked by Pat Gibson

Photograph No 3 (FIG 4.30)
looking at the photograph
(Fig 4.30), our eight-year-old
thought this was the same as
the previous one. There is a
very subtle difference, which
does show in the worked lace.
If there is a large space to fill,
the two stitches worked in the
same area makes a good
variation.

Foundation row of spaced
stitches

1st row 6 stitches into each
long loop

2nd row 2 stitches between the
groups of 6, 1 stitch each side
of the 2 centre stitches of the
group of 6 above

3rd row 2 stitches each side of
the pairs of stitches, 1 between
the 2 centre stitches of the
group of 5

4th row 1 stitch between the
pairs, which leaves a long loop
between 5 stitches

5th row Back to the 6 stitches
into each long loop, as in the
1st row

Photograph No 4 (FIG 4.31)

Foundation row 2 stitches with
a space of 2 across the row

1st row 2 stitches into each
long loop between the sets of 2
and cord back

2nd row 1 stitch between the
sets of 2 and 2 over each long
loop worked over the cord

3rd row 1 stitch between the 2
stitches worked over the long
loop, which brings you back
to the 1st row

Photograph No 5 (FIG 4.32)

Foundation row Work 4
stitches, leave a space of 3,
work 3 stitches leave a space
of 3. 4 stitches space of 3
across the row

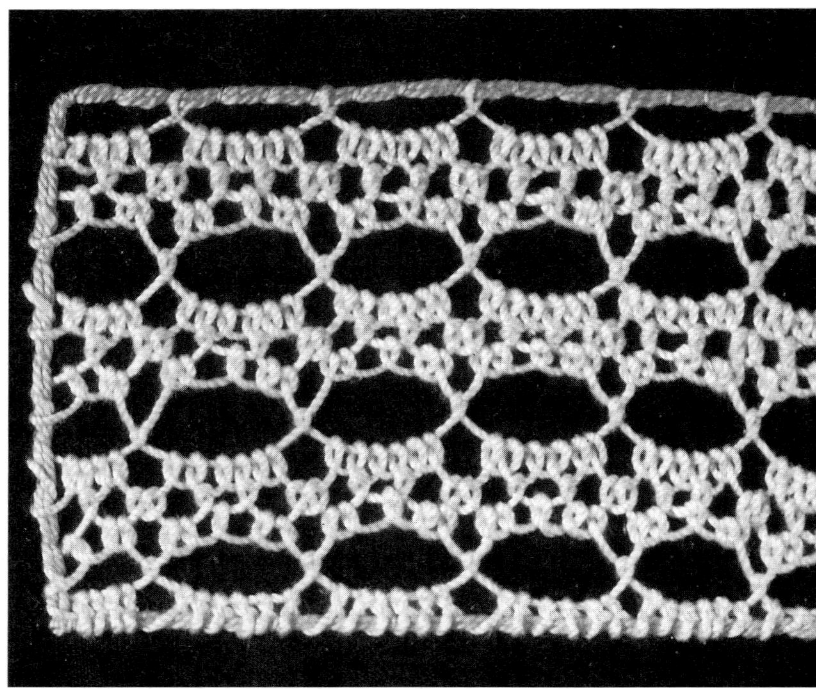

FIG 4.30 Variation on Fig 4.29

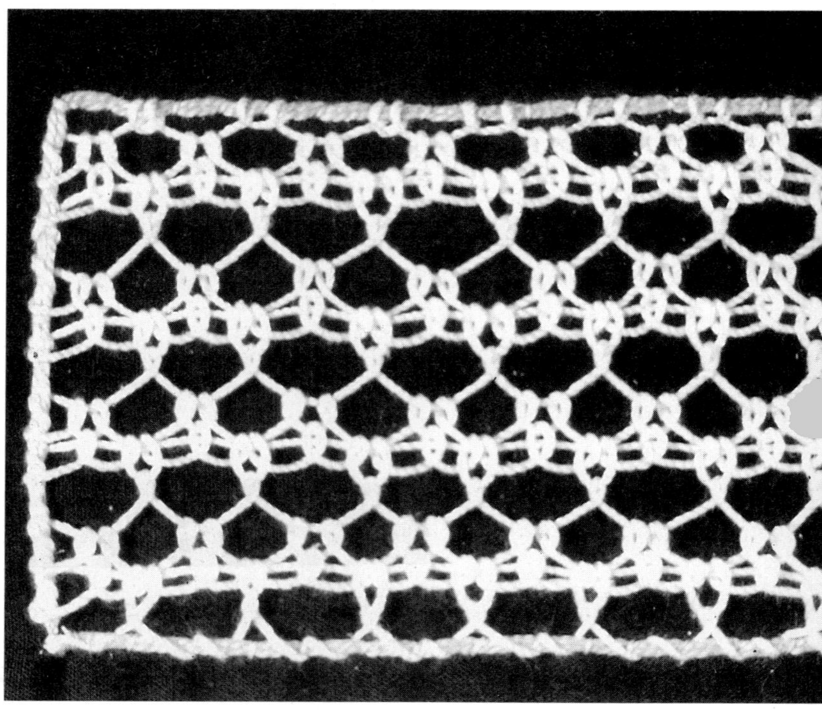

FIG 4.31 Variation on the Pea Stitch

1st row This is made up of 9 stitches in blocks of 3 leaving a space of 3 stitches between blocks. Work the 9 stitches in this way: 3 stitches are worked into the loop between the blocks of 3 and 4 of the foundation row. 3 stitches are worked into the loops of the blocks of 4, then work 3 stitches into the next loop, this makes up the 9 stitches. Miss 3 stitches and work the next block of 9 stitches in the same way

2nd row Make 3 stitches into the loops of the last 4 stitches of the first block of 9, make 3 stitches into the loop between the blocks of 9 of the previous row, then 3 stitches into the loops of the first 4 stitches of the next block of 9. Now you have to leave the 3 centre stitches of the block of 9 of the previous row and start the next block of 9 in the same way

3rd row The same as the 1st row, making the blocks of 9 stitches with a loop under the middle stitches of the 9 on the row above

4th row The same as the foundation row, block of 4, long loop, block of 3, long loop, block of 4, etc. across the row

Photograph No 6 (FIG 4.33)

Foundation row Blocks of 3 with space of 4 between

1st row Work 2 stitches on the loops of the blocks of 3 of the foundation row

2nd row Work 2 stitches on the loop of the pair of stitches of the previous row. Work 2 stitches over the loops of the last 2 rows and continue across row

3rd row Work 3 stitches into the loop of the pairs of stitches (not those over the 2 rows) and repeat from row 1

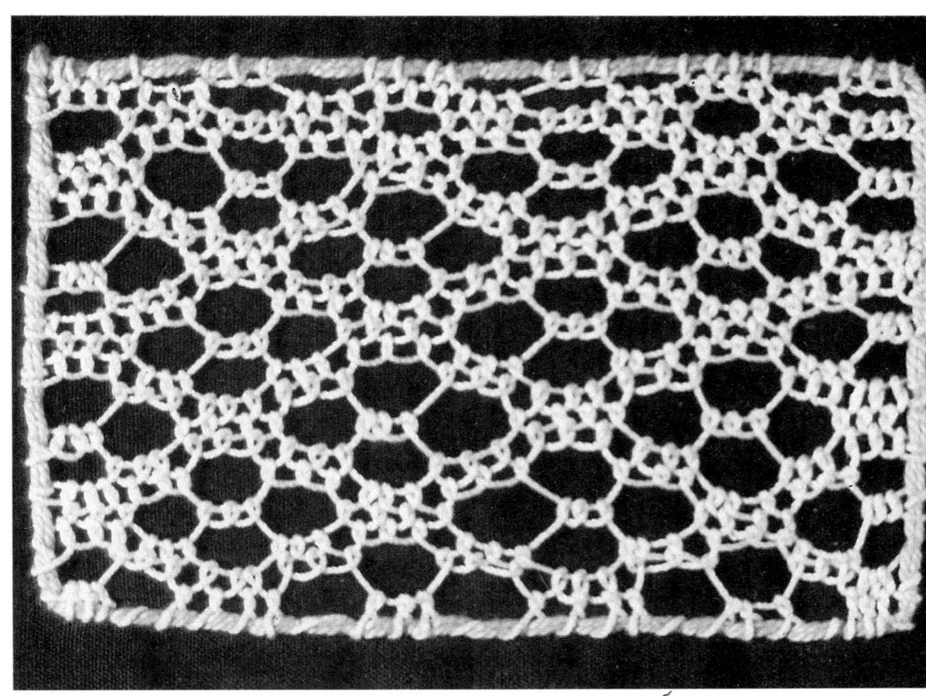

FIG 4.32 Four-hole bud

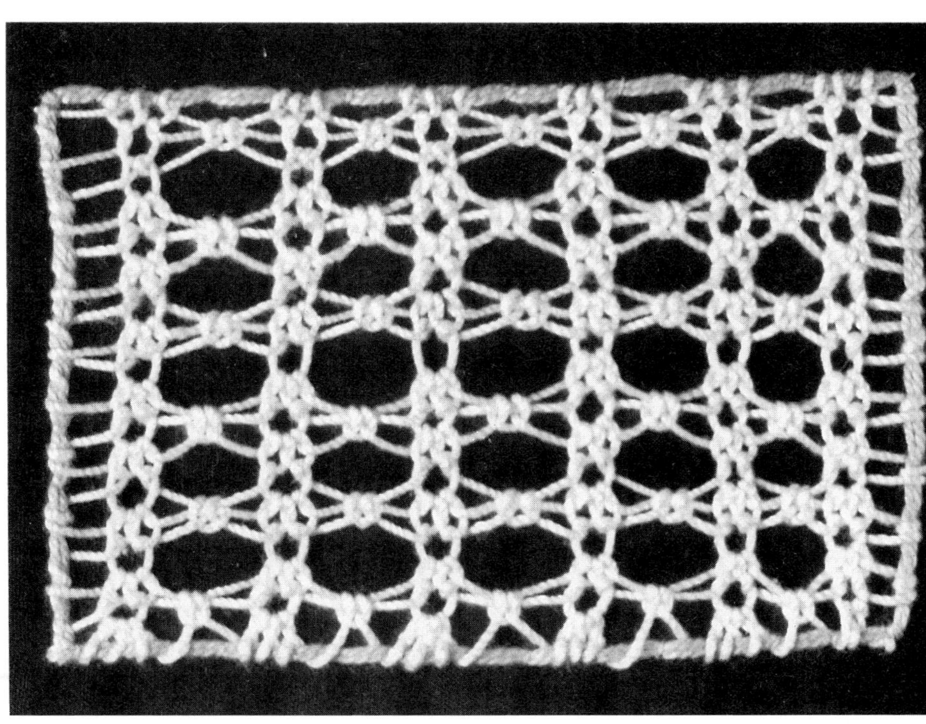

FIG 4.33 Ground from an old piece of Flemish lace

Photograph No 7 (FIG 4.34)

Foundation row 1 stitch and the space of 4 across the row

1st row Into each long loop work 4 stitches

2nd row Into the loops of the blocks of 4 of the previous row work 3 stitches

3rd row Into each loop of the 3 work 2 stitches, take the needle back and work a stitch just before the first of those 2 stitches and on the loop just made work 5 stitches. Now work the next 2 stitches into the loops of the next block of 3 and repeat.

That is *Belle Point de Venise* and can be worked as a pattern on its own (said our eight-your-old). You must then repeat the foundation row to start off on the pattern again.

In the photograph, 2 extra rows have been added to give more substance to the lace, as it is easier to see where you are in the pattern. The first of the extra rows consists of 6 stitches into each long row. The 2nd row has 5 stitches worked into the loops of the 6 on the row above.

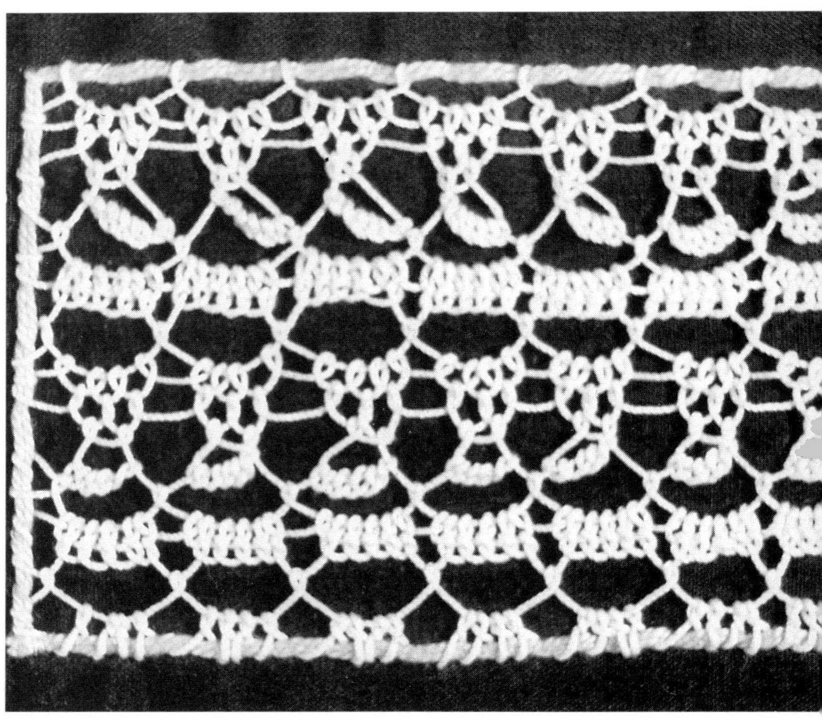

FIG 4.34 *Belle Toile* Ground

5

The four seasons

There's always some tree ornament
of which we never tire,
A shiny ball, an angel
or a graceful silver spire.
Though others may be broken
this one is kept from year to year,
it always makes the Christmas tree
more beautiful and dear.

And so it is with friendship,
for each life is like a tree
and the ornaments that trim it,
show how lovely it can be.

There is Nina's Tree of grand-daughters' names
and Cathy's pristine star,
Daphne's little bauble
and beautiful they are.

Life's ornaments are blessings
and they may be great or small,
But the blessing of true friendship
is the dearest one of all.

So many friends found time to work on this book, so this is dedicated to each and every one of them. Doreen, Maureen, Winnie and of course, my children and my grandchildren are my greatest friends of all.

The four seasons

As far as children were concerned life was one long holiday, according to Mother. So some holidays just had to be more holiday than others, according to my reckoning. Christmas for instance – it wasn't every day of the week that the house smelt of mince pies, turkey roasting and the wonderful smell of Mull. For those of you who have never tasted good old-fashioned mull, you will have to use your imagination. Think about wine, spices, egg yolks, brown sugar, rum and floating around on top of this delicious concoction three or four oranges spiked all over with cloves. This would be warming on the top of the kitchen hob. It was enough to resuscitate all the bees and wasps from hibernation. Thinking back, it had the opposite effect on the men, as it put them all to sleep. The point proved yet again, as the women were so busy preparing, laying up, and keeping the children out of the presents and from wrecking the Christmas tree, that they never had time to drink enough to even feel drowsy.

FIG 5.1 Cathy's star

FIG 5.2 The grand-daughters' tree

FIG 5.3 The bear who came down from the tree. Work him in Double Point de Venise to get a crunchy look. The ball needs to be smooth, so that can be worked in Corded Stitch

Mother had it all wrong about life being one long holiday, as it was ages from Christmas to Easter. Easter, now that was something extra special to me, for it would mean many things, such as bonnets with lace and buttercups. Yes, really, Easter was when everything became new again. We used to have sunshine and warm weather, which meant our summer clothes came out of moth balls. There were Easter eggs with painted faces, chocolate ones, Simnel cake awash with almond paste, hot-cross-buns and going backwards and forwards to Church so many times there was hardly time to eat any of it. Flowers filled the Church with scent. The Arum lillies reminded me of funerals, because ladies in the flower shop made rings of them, then left them to die in the Churchyard on a mound of bare earth. It would make much more sense, it seemed to me, to put the lillies in a vase of water on the landing table and not have a funeral. But in Church at Easter, there were vases of Winter sweet, Narcissi and Orange Blossom with a smell so thick it stopped your brain from going any further. I had not a clue as to what the sermon was all about, as my head was so full of 'smell'. On arriving home I did remember to tell Grandma that an Easter smell would make a beautiful design for lace, but I did not tell her about the music design. I had already been smacked for that once. You see, having spent most of the morning working out how to make a design from smells, something else filled my head.

FIG 5.4a This swan was designed
and worked by Nina Devereux
He really looks as if he is about to
chat up a lady swan

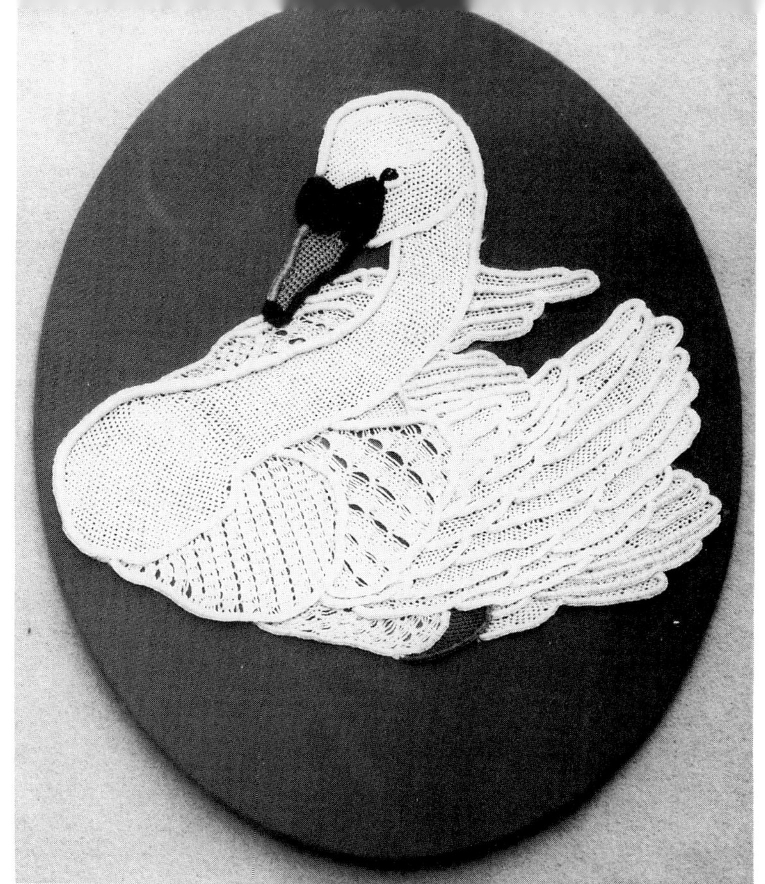

FIG 5.4b Daphne's little bauble
that the cat had a game with
before we were able to
photograph it

The choir and the organ between them, were making a design for an extra beautiful lace. It would have to be needlepoint, and only Venetian would be round enough and strong enough to be that beautiful. It was the *Messiah*: the boy's voices would trill the couronnes, the men would swell the cordonnette, the organ was making the most perfect background – I could almost picture it finished. Then, wallop, my hand was smacked for day-dreaming, when I should have stood up to sing like everyone else. It was a lovely, lovely day-dream.

Leaving Easter behind, there used to be a thing called Empire Day. All the men with their medals and sticks would march through The High, while all the children wore white and carried Union flags for the 'march past'. I was never sure quite what they marched past – being small, I must have missed it. There was always picnic lunch with lots of lemonade and then in the afternoon it was Sports Day. How was one supposed to run after gallons of lemonade? Just to jump up and down made little girls' tummies bubble. Then everyone else received prizes, *Land of Hope and Glory* was sung and the rest of the day was a holiday. May Day

FIG 5.6 Which came first? The chicken and egg

was a holiday too: that was when you had to plait ribbons round the Maypole. You had to skip round the thing saying, one to the left, one to the right. Then as long as everyone stopped at the right time and turned round the other way, it was one to the right and one to the left. Those skipping in the opposite direction had to remember to say it back to front. I always managed to remember it wrong, was always in trouble afterwards, and always blamed it on to my short fat legs. Mother said it was my bird brain, but I did not care too much, as I could plait with any number of ribbons in my hands when I was on my own. It was the others who made the Maypole go awry.

So each year Christmas came and went, as did Easter, Empire Day and May Day. The long summer holiday meant the London trip and visit to the other Grandparents.

So through to Michaelmas, when there was always a fair – not the sort of fair that you have now. You were lucky if there was a merry-go-round and swings to be allowed on. The fair then was all about dressing up in pretty dresses, and being allowed to stay up late into the night to watch the dancing on the green; to smell the

Hot Potato oven, and even maybe to have a hot potato which was given in squares of newspaper, which is why I was not allowed one unless Father was there – Mother would not let you eat out of newspaper. There was always the rock stall with barley sugar sticks, aniseed balls, twists of liquorice and glass walking-sticks of hundreds and thousands, and – dare I mention it – Gob Stoppers. Needless to say, these too were banned unless Mother was well out of sight. They went on and on until, right in the middle, you bit into an aniseed ball. Would you believe there were white and pink sugar mice with long string tails which gave me the creeps.

After Michaelmas was Guy Fawkes night and then Christmas. It may seem a funny way to tell the seasons, but to me that is how the year progressed, through smells and music and happenings all of which reminded me of lace. Let us see how the seasons of the sea can give beautiful designs for lace, how your mind can run riot over Easter, and Christmasses long since past. This book is of memories of lace.

FIG 5.7 Easter Fantasy

9. Spring Tides. Designed by Nina Devereux and worked by the Author using the same Chinese silks and Madeira metallic threads

10. Summer Sands. Designed and worked by Pippa Louise in Gütermann 100/3s and Madeira threads

11. Autumn Seas. Designed and worked by the
Author using the Chinese silks, Gütermann 100/3s,
and Madeira metallic threads

12. Winter Storms. Designed and worked by the
Author. The threads are the same as used for the
previous two designs. This is a twin to the
photograph shown in Ros Hills' book *Colour and
Texture in Needlelace*. This time it is worked entirely
in needlelace stitches

13. Easter Flowers. Designed by Elicia and worked by Doreen Holmes

14. The Maypole. Worked by the adult students from Kemp Welch School, Poole, Dorset

15. The Pony Who Escaped From The Carousel. Designed by Zaien and worked by Winnie Hunt using Gütermann 100/3s

16. Fox Cub. Designed and worked by
Kate Marie especially for this book. The
toadstools were cultivated by Vera
Nicholls

17. Flower Fairies. Designed and
worked by Nina Devereux

FIG 5.8 This is how Elicia
visualised the 'flowers that filled
the Church with smell' Clematis,
freesia and jonquils

105

FIG 5.9 An escape from the
Merry-go-Round. A design from
Zaien worked by Winnie Hunt

FIG 5.10 Spring Tides. When the Nerides swim along the Gulf Stream

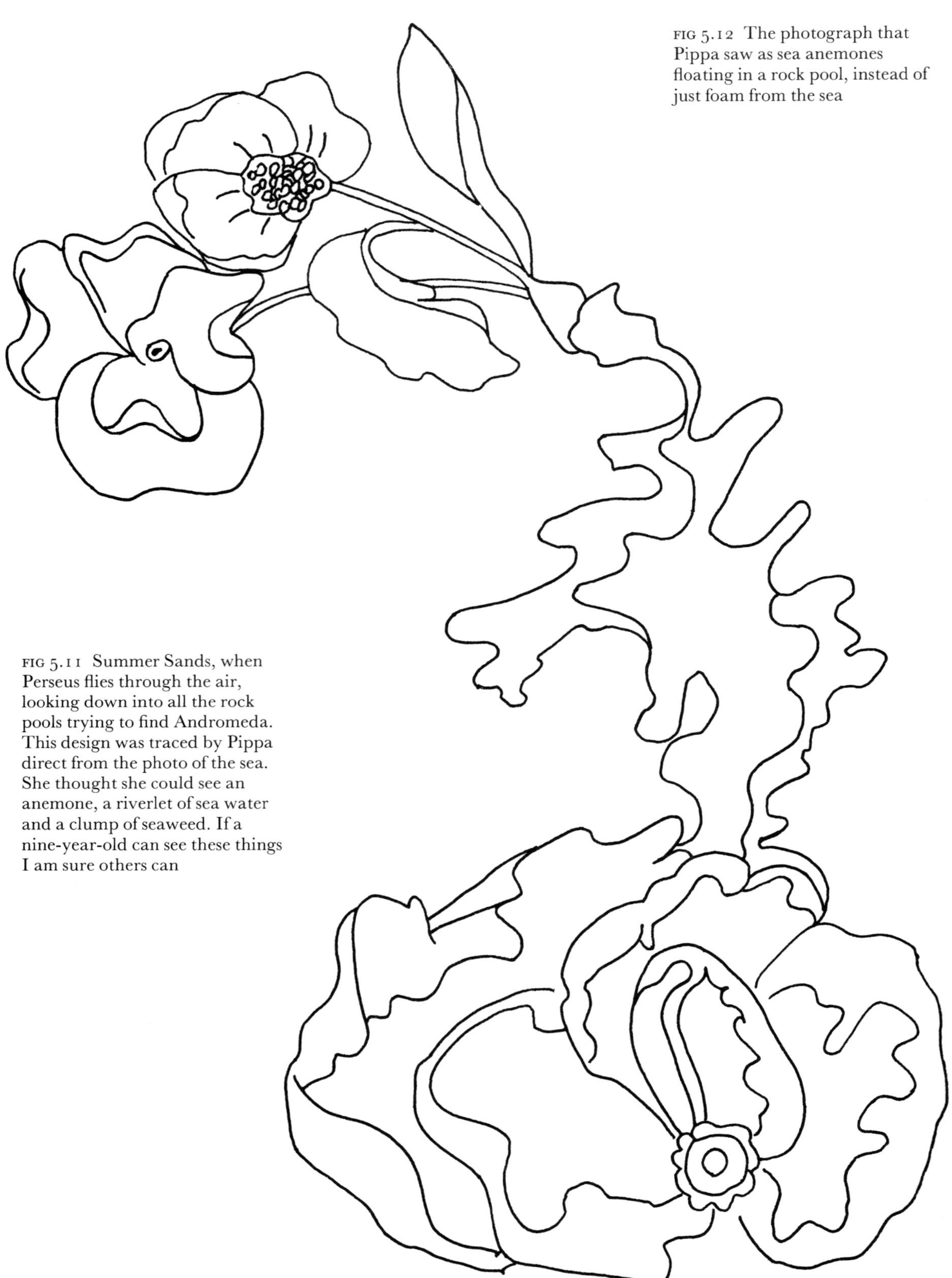

FIG 5.12 The photograph that
Pippa saw as sea anemones
floating in a rock pool, instead of
just foam from the sea

FIG 5.11 Summer Sands, when
Perseus flies through the air,
looking down into all the rock
pools trying to find Andromeda.
This design was traced by Pippa
direct from the photo of the sea.
She thought she could see an
anemone, a riverlet of sea water
and a clump of seaweed. If a
nine-year-old can see these things
I am sure others can

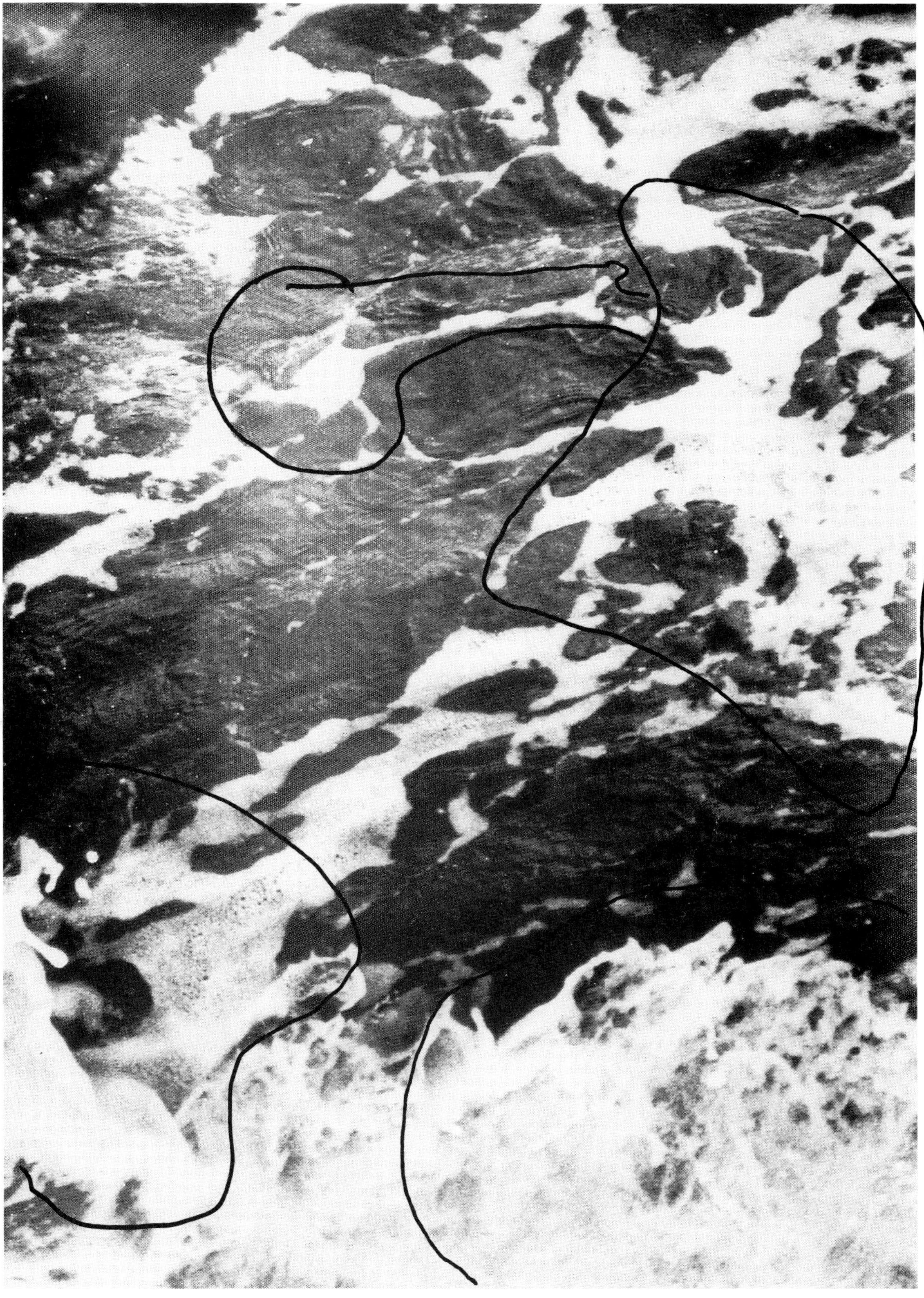

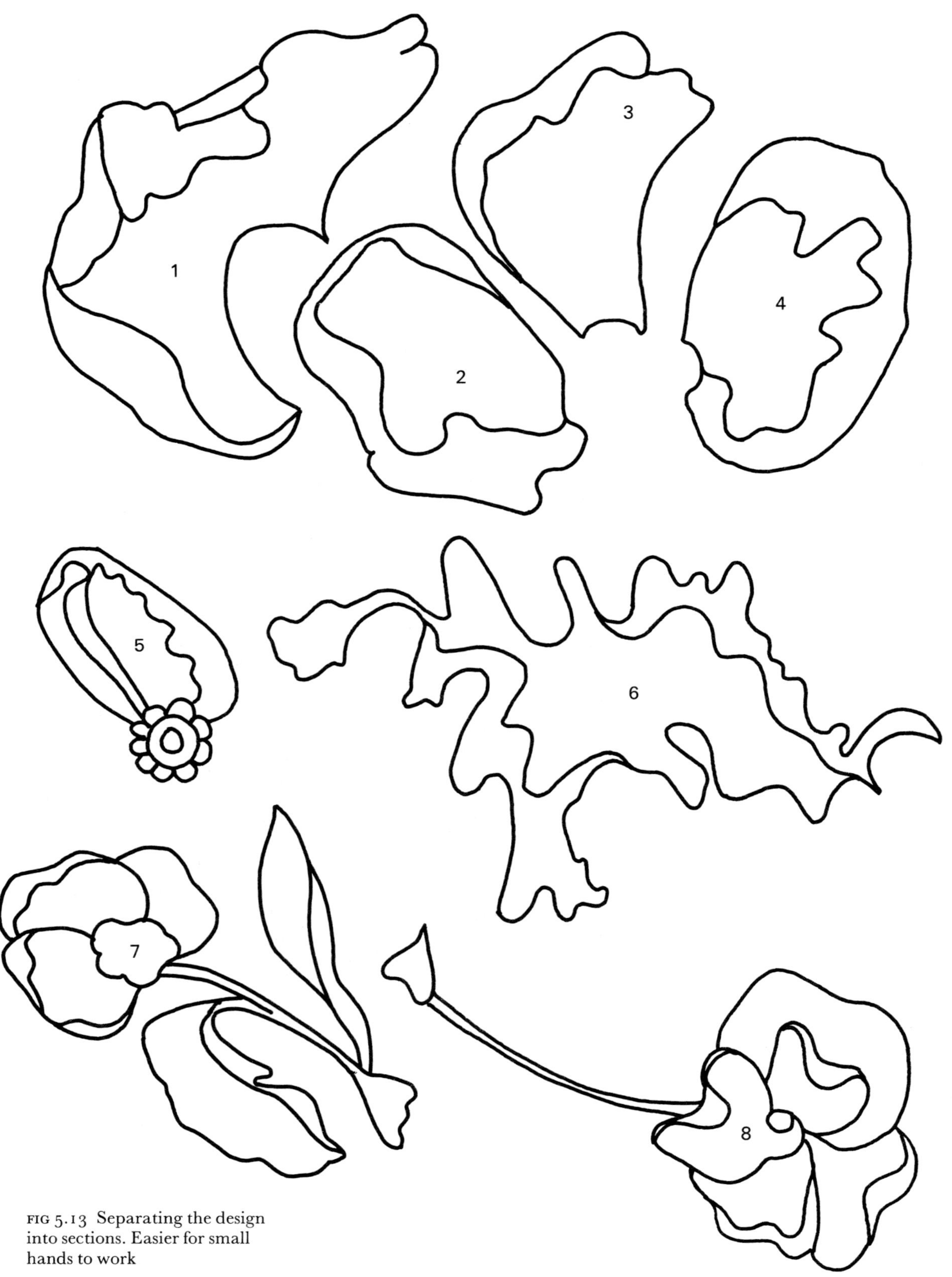

FIG 5.13 Separating the design
into sections. Easier for small
hands to work

FIG 5.15 Winter Storm.
Poseidon, surveying his kingdom
of the seas

6
Growing pains

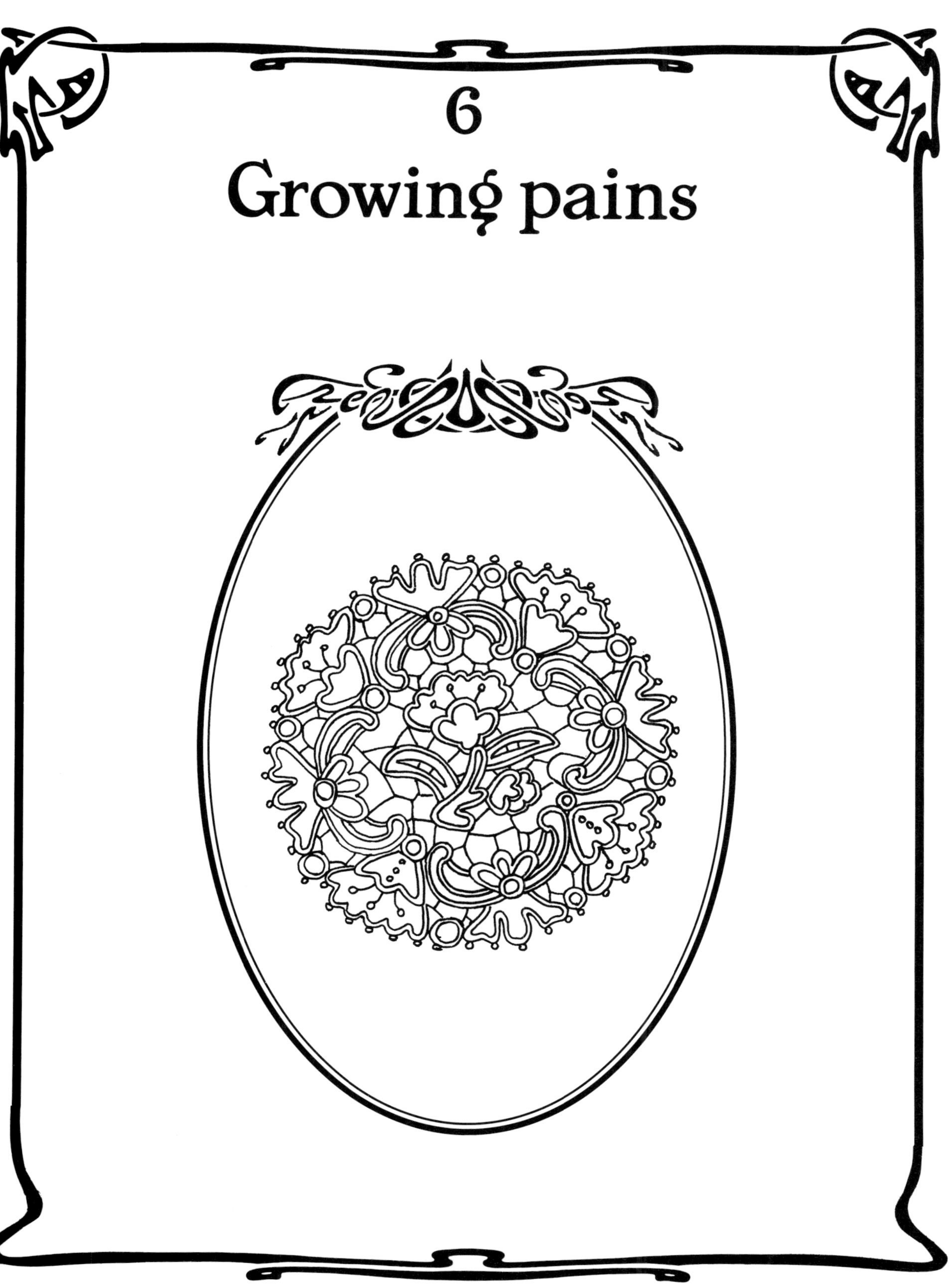

FIG 6.1 This is a view of Chain Pier Lodge. As you can see, it was tucked right into the cliff. If you look closely you will see the balcony – it shows up black, as it had shutters that could be pulled together if the weather was rough. It was a great place to stand to drop maggots on to the unsuspecting folks below

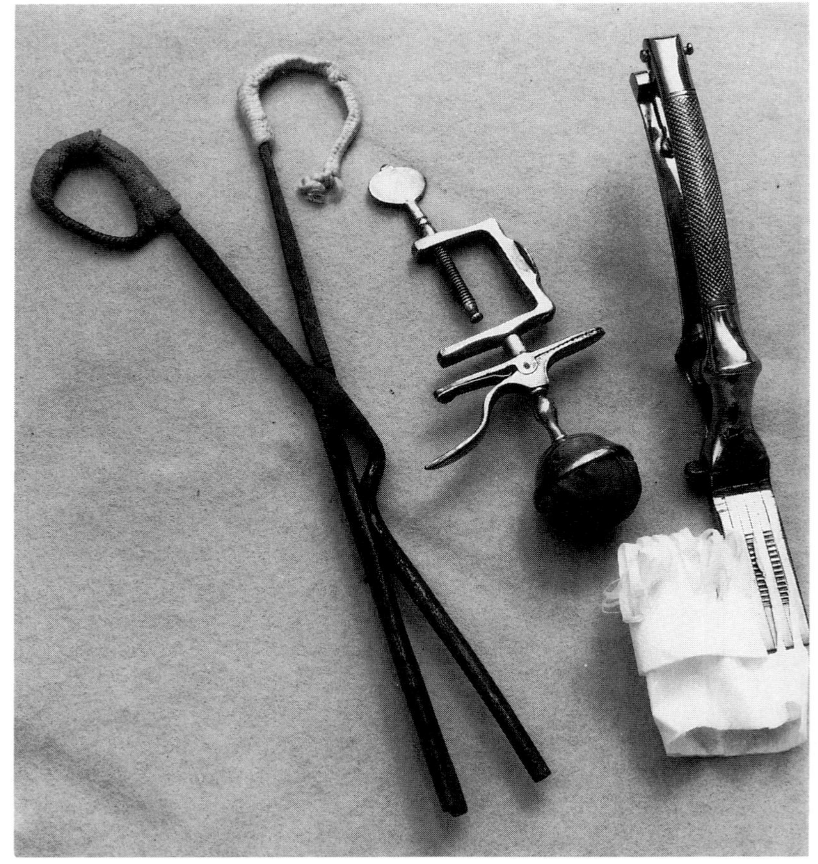

FIG 6.2 A goffering iron, a Cutlet Frill cutter and the little silver sewing clamp

It was decided that I was now old enough to go away on holiday alone. As there was an Aunt who lived in Brighton, Sussex, that was where I was sent, 'Care of the Guard', on a steam train to London, where I was met by Grandfather. Then, 'Care of the Guard' again, on another train to Brighton. Aunt did not live in an ordinary house. Hers was called Chain Pier Lodge, and at one time it had been part of the Pier. It was built into the rock of the cliffs along Maderia Drive, and if you stood on the balcony, with the glass partitions open, it was possible to feel the spray on your face if the sea was high and rough. I had a secret game here too; it was to offer to shell the peas, and collect all the maggots off them in a match box, go out onto the balcony, and drop the maggots onto the hats of the people strolling along on what was called the Promenade.

One year during my stay there the fashion was for Beach Pyjamas and all the ladies wore them. Aunt made me a pair and I was allowed to walk so far one way and then so far the other along the 'Prom', while Aunt watched from above. I really thought that I was growing up.

There are two main memories of Brighton holidays. The first was when I was almost eight. Aunt was engaged to be married to a Mounted Policeman and a very grand-looking man he was, sitting astride his big black horse called Stirling. There were plans for a wedding dress of silk with a handkerchief skirt which would hang in three layers, one below the other. But the Mounted Policeman was hurt and died. At first I thought he too would vanish on Monday and come back Saturday, but dying was something different from working. They tried to explain, but it seemed to me that you went from one boring thing to something even more boring.

The unfinished wedding dress lay for ages in tissue paper in a drawer. I would often creep into the room, open the drawer and run my fingers through the silk. There was nothing else in the world so beautiful. All the bottom layer of the skirt and part of the middle layer was finished. There was uncut silk and a large length of lace. Aunt was too sad to look at it. Within a day or two the holiday ended and I had to go home. The next time Aunt came to visit she brought the unfinished dress with her, and on one unforgettable day Aunt said 'Let's make the girls a dress each from that silk', as she was sure she would never ever need another wedding dress. The dresses began to look like butterflies, hanging up between fittings, and during the times Mother worked on the material. There was enough in the large square for three layers for my dress and enough in the other square for three layers for little sister. The uncut silk made the bodices and sleeves. Then came the Sunday when we actually wore the dresses. I found that, if I could twist around fast enough, the layers of the skirt floated out around me so that it felt as if I was floating on a cloud. Little sister, now called Louise, couldn't turn round fast without toppling over so she would pick up the top layer of her dress and put it over her head; she was so blonde and pretty that she looked like a Princess.

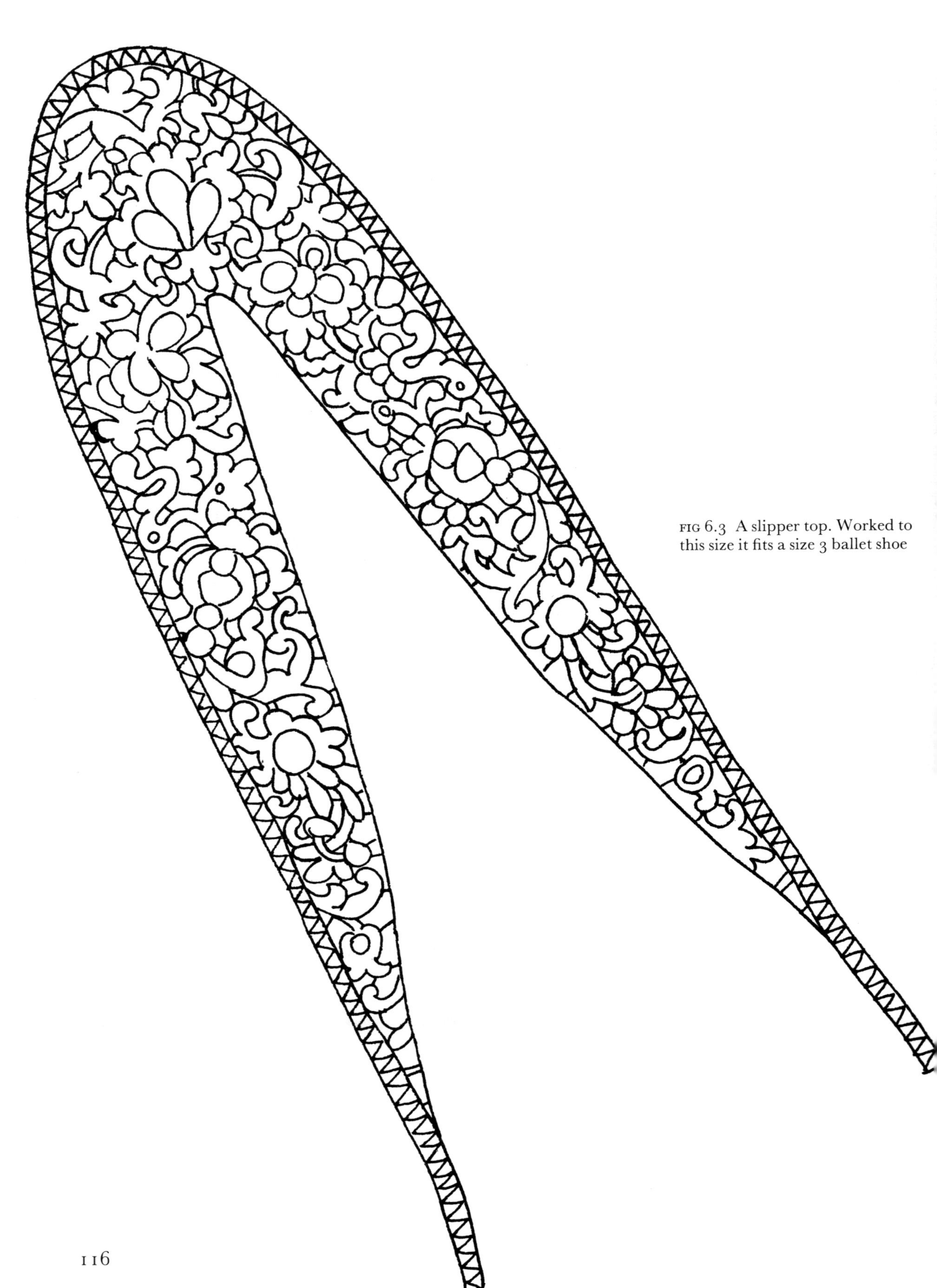

FIG 6.3 A slipper top. Worked to this size it fits a size 3 ballet shoe

FIG 6.4a The Bride. The dress is made of white voile with a bobbin lace edge round the four layers of the skirt. The sleeve flounces and the collar are made from antique Flemish lace, to give her something old, while the waistcoat was made in Tambour lace, along with the sprays on skirt, by Joan Merifield, to give her something new. Her underclothes have ribbons of blue. The veil has scrolls and roses of Honiton lace; her petticoat has a wide band of white work. Maybe she is more a stitch sampler than a bride

FIG 6.4b The wedding cake was made by members of the Wokingham Lace Makers; the doilies are of bobbin lace and the medallions are needlepoint. It was worked for the Lace Guild 1987 Exhibition and was at each of the venues

FIG 6.5 The bolero pattern which is worked as Tambour lace for the 'Bride' by Joan Merifield

FIG 6.6 Silver sewing clamp,
complete with pincushion

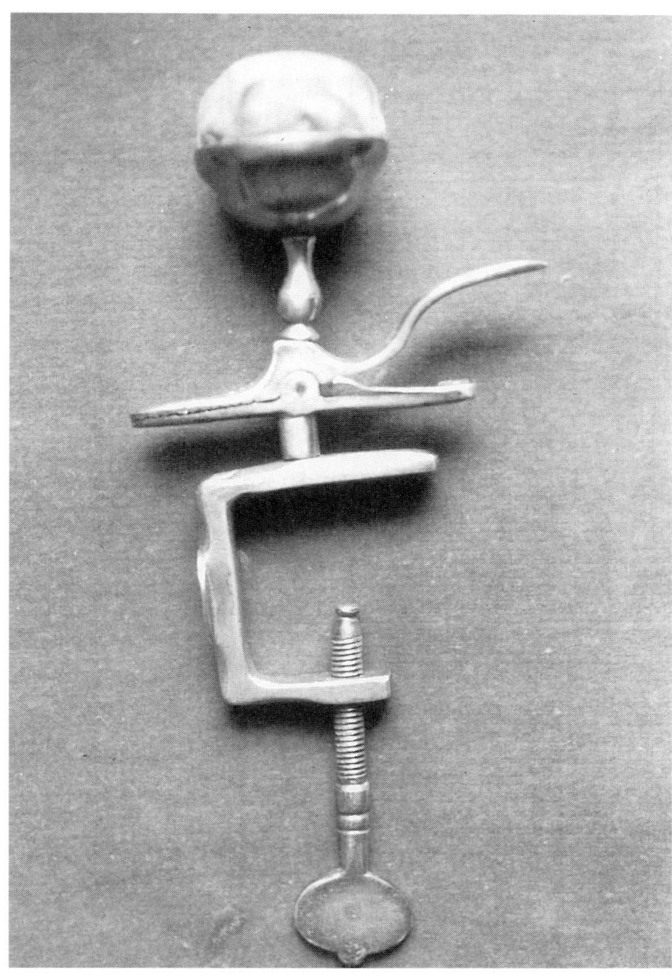

FIG 6.7 For looking down noses
at little girls while attending
garden parties, these little
Lorgnettes have a terrific
magnification

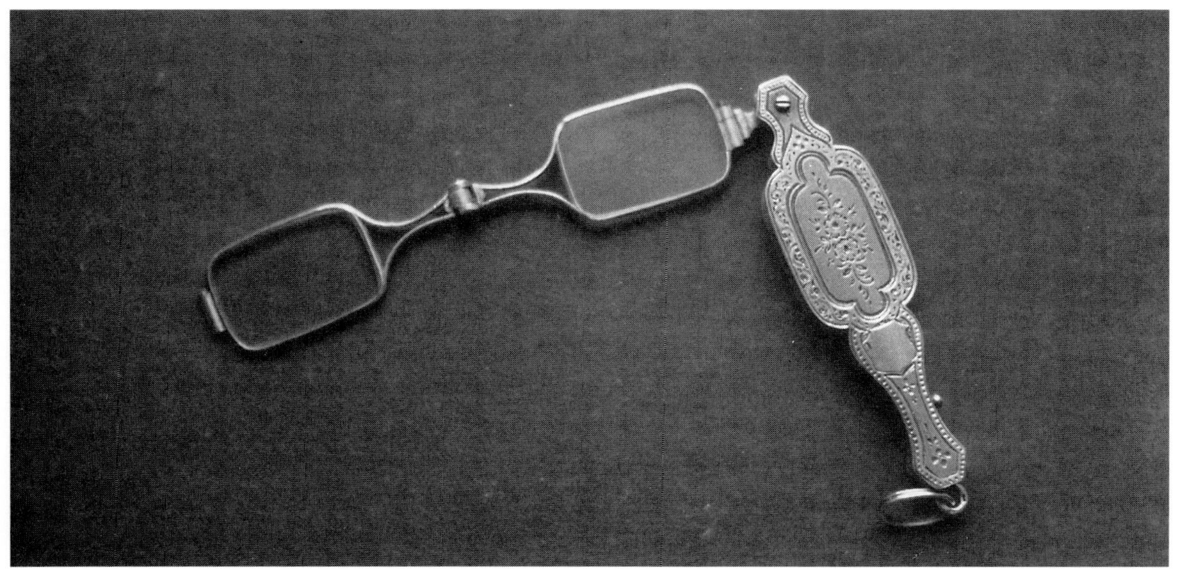

FIG 6.8 One half of the front of a nightdress top. A pattern for Tambour lace

FIG 6.9 One half of the back and shoulder of the nightdress

FIG 6.10 A drawing of a head-dress designed for grand-daughter Kate Marie for her First Communion

My next visit was at around the age of nine. This was the first time in my life that I was forced to think about growing up. First, I was taken to one of the private tea parties held on the lawn of the Royal Pavilion. That was the first time I had ever seen Ladies holding their glasses on the end of long handles. When they put them on their noses they seemed to have to put their heads back so far it was a wonder they ever saw the child below. They did, and many an arched eyebrow could be seen, as they met another pair of eyes behind a pair of glasses. Certainly I had the feeling that I should never have been there.

The most exciting part was being taken in to one of the apartments to be shown some of the most beautiful lace and silk underwear that the owner of the apartment was wearing for her 'London Season'. It was the sheer volume of clothes as much as the beauty of each piece that confounded me. How could anyone have enough drawers to put it all away? Aunt explained that it was hung up, and never folded except between layers of tissue paper, otherwise the silk would crack along the folds. So little rouleau bands were sewn into everything to hang them up and all the lacy French knickers were folded in tissue before being put away. There was a lady called May who hovered in the background, getting all this stuff out and putting it back after it had been admired. There was so much lace scattered around that room; I just wondered who could have made so much for one lady.

Aunt explained that it came from a *Salon* in France and there were ladies who worked all day and half the night sitting at their pillows, making lace for this fashion house. They received very little money for all this work, and it seems they were all getting old and the young girls would not work for so little money.

Lace was so lovely that to sit and make it all day could hardly be called work, so why did the young girls need money? I made it for love. On the way home in a taxi, something I had never been in before, Aunt tried to tell me about the business side of lace-making. To live, it seemed, takes money. To make lace to live does not leave any money for the others to take.

Horrid little warning bells started to ring in my head. I was remembering things back home – only little things, because I was considered too young to be included in grown-up talk. But snatches of conversation seeped into my head: the discussion about the current price of thread that was sent overland from Spain, and how the lace could be made on a more economical basis. I did not understand quite what it was all about, but could picture Grandma drawing comical, funny designs.

Then I remembered a whispered secret that I had overheard. Mother and Grandma talking about Great Grand Mother. 'She really did want to continue working, but it was a strain on her at her age'. It was time the two conspirators took more of the workload between them and left her to redesign the pattern books. Thinking about it, that is what Great Grand Mother had been doing for quite a while. One other thought came to me on that long journey home. Mother had said that her daughter would be the

designer, not the one who plied the needle or worked the bobbins; that way she could get into the big fashion houses in London. It was all part of growing up, into a grown-up's world, and I did not like the sound of it one bit.

Once home, my ears were to the ground all the time trying to catch up with this new economy thing that seemed to be the main topic of conversation.

It is funny how little things change on the broad spectrum of life. I wonder what on earth I would have thought if I could have looked into a crystal ball and seen myself in that adult world. An old wrinkled prune, sitting at a word processor, scribbling my thoughts and memories, and drawing designs on a computer with a thing called a light pen. In those far-off days I would not even have understood what electricity was, as even the wireless worked on a cat's whisker. What an age away my last stay at Brighton as a child seems. I watched the R101 airship float out across the sea on its way to France. I had been taken up in an aeroplane with only a belt and a rubber apron to keep me from falling out. It had cost five whole shillings for a flight of sheer terror! I was told that the plane had a rubber band which wound the propellor up tight when the 'driver' turned it round before 'take-off'. When the rubber band unwound the plane would fall down, and it was out over the sea heading for Black Rock: I was unable to think which I would sooner fall down on, or in. I can only remember twisting an imaginary rubber band all the time I was up there, and being told to look over there somewhere, where I would see France. My eyes were so tightly shut I only felt the wind in my hair and my ears being deafened by the engine, while I just waited for the rubber band to snap.

In 1929 Great Grandmother died very suddenly. There was much sadness and many long discussions on how life would be rearranged. There were numerous lace contracts to be honoured, and I was now old enough to help in small ways.

It was much better pinning out lace for its final press, or laying it in tissue paper ready for delivery, than looking after a baby brother and a toddler sister.

Then by the end of the year Grandma died. That really was the biggest blow and to help compensate for the dreadful loss, Mother let me take her last length of work off the pillow. It was a beautiful flounce of Honiton that she had taken over from Great Grandmother. It was still unfinished, with pieces of the sprigs that made up the design all in their separate little boxes. For a while I tried to continue it, but the tears always smudged things up and it was not possible to see where the needle was going. This lace was also wrapped up in tissue, and is to this day still the most beautiful piece of lace I have.

FIG 6.12 The River Thames and playing 'Ducks and Drakes'

Life went on, in a different kind of way. Mrs Moss appeared to have moved into our house and took over all the household duties, leaving Mother to bring all the work up to date. I spent more and more time trying to help, and became very efficient at making rolled edges along the yards of chiffon hems. Somehow it was never work, nor was the stocktaking when Mother showed me how to do that. It was no longer mother and daughter, but two people working together. Soon I could arrange the engrelure for collars, as well as flounces. The best was still to come, when at long last I was allowed to do the 'sprigging'. Then we all knew I was 'one of them'.

The talk was all 'house-hunting', something that had never entered the conversation before. Visits away to 'foreign' parts, at one point to Buckinghamshire, were contemplated, but it was decided that it should be Surrey.

We moved to a new home. Never again was I to lay on my bed and watch the sunlight hit the sea and send rippling patterns across the ceiling. This was Surrey and nobody here made lace; they all thought it came from Nottingham. Rosa and Louisa Tebbs had retired; the only thing worth going to London for was to visit the Victoria and Albert Museum. Even 'Albert', still standing on top of his stairs, was no longer as big and there were certainly not as many steps to get up to him as I remembered. It is true the older one gets the smaller things become, and Albert was no exception.

Things like Mrs Moss, Willie's girl, her brother Thom and the girl who 'did' were now nothing but dreams. There were good things in life after one was eleven: having the River Thames almost in the back garden; Hampton Court Palace, where you could practise being a lady, walking down the main stairway without holding the ballustrade and keeping your nose at an angle so that, if you had to wear glasses, they would never fall off. Keeping your teeth together when speaking to try to copy the Surrey accent. Being entered for Art School. There is nothing that brings you down quicker than growing up. Now the talk was scholarships – would the money ever allow for school fees if the subject of the conversation could not pass her exams; was the subject really as good in the wide world as everyone thought she was in the small world of country education? Maybe she proved better than was feared. The College was free, but the books, etc, were not.

Mother joined the WI and was approached by the Institute to start lace classes in the area. Soon, lace classes were springing up like mushrooms and there was to become a new type of lacemaker. There were many new books on the subject and Coats would supply bobbins and thread by post. No longer did we have to wait for the supplier from Spain. No longer were there Buying Days nor, if I remember rightly, was there any port in those crystal glasses! No longer did people sit at their lace until the small hours of each morning, trying to get an order finished; now they plied their bobbins for the pleasure of making lace.

There were now other Colleges to aim for, and at this point in my life I was introduced to the Royal School of Needlework.

A lot of water has flowed under many bridges since those far-off days. Many of my students have been infected with the lace fever; some will never get over the effects. Now my grand-daughters are suffering to some degree.

All through the 1930s lace tried to make a comeback, but the Second World War put paid to that, as there was not much time for such niceties after 1939. I do remember making lace while off-duty, sitting in a dug-out in Plymouth; also showing a crowd of Canadians how it was made while stationed on the Isle of Dogs, in London, between the doodle-bugs and black-out. When our station in Crosby, Liverpool, received a direct hit, we ended up in New Brighton on the other side of the Mersey. We were in appalling little huts and there I held a class for bobbin lace which lasted six weeks. It was not quite the type of lace you would expect, because we used bandages for threads, which were drawing-

FIG 6.13 Fox cub designed and worked by Kate Marie

pinned across the hut windows and Torchon-stitched into place, each row being fixed with other drawing-pins into the wood of the window. It was finished off with the shells from the beach which were tied to the ends of each bandage. It looked quite smart and we were presented with a medal made of red sealing wax for our efforts. The trouble with that was it snapped into fragments because it was so brittle; even so, it was my first award for making lace.

Then I was married. Remember those two triangles? Well, there really were six little triangles. My six children had to grow up before I could surface again.

In 1967 I started my own Craft Centre in a converted brewery. Not licensed premises, I might add, and very dry. The members were offered lapidary, silversmithing and enamelling and, on another floor, well away from the mess, there was spinning, weaving, embroidery and the biggest and most popular classes? Lace. At the last count, in 1973, some 300 students had been infected with the lace fever. Many have become tutors of lace as far away as India, New Zealand, Canada and the USA.

Some very well-known lace makers were once my students, as were two other young ladies before they became my Daughters-in-Law and your Mothers. You even have Fathers who can spin, weave, and earn their living drawing or making gold and silver ware, so you dare not let me down.

Saint Francis of Assisi said

> He who works with his hands is a labourer,
> He who works with his hands and his head is a craftsman,
> He who works with his hands, and his head and his heart is an artist.

May I add to that by saying, all this and compassion too, will turn you into a Saint.

FIG 6.14a Fuchsia and butterfly.
Designed and worked by Daphne
Keen using Gütermann 100/3s
silk and Madeira Metallic
threads

FIG 6.14b Not sitting pretty in
their own eggs, the Bruges-type
swan and the butterfly were
worked by the Author, the
decorated eggs were made by
Avril Rimmer

A Local Challenge to the Machine Age

The Berkshire Crafts Centre at Wokingham

By Janet Walford

IN an age of increasing mass production, when hand-made goods are rapidly becoming things of the past, the Berkshire Crafts Centre comes as a breath of fresh air. Here are taught the crafts that our forefathers practised — spinning, lacemaking, weaving, tatting, basketry, crocheting, enamelling. They are arts that are in danger of dying out in this busy modern world of ours, and the object of the Crafts Centre is to save them.

Wokingham is the headquarters of the Centre; and although it only opened in April there are already 115 enthusiastic members, including one in Canada ! People travel regularly to it from as far as Aylesbury, Oxford and Ashford (Middlesex); and one person who attends hopes to open a similar centre when she returns to her home in New Zealand.

The atmosphere is friendly and relaxed, and students learn by helping each other as well as through their instructors. Lapiduary work, pewter work, embroidery and tapestry are also taught besides those crafts already mentioned.

The founder of the Centre was Mrs. Nena Lovesey, who is now its principal, and she insists, "It is time I was left out of the story. The Centre is run by a committee. The chairman is a lecturer at Reading University, and members of the committee include an accountant, a bank manager and a solicitor."

Without Mrs. Lovesey however, there would be no Crafts Centre and no story to tell. The project was the culmination of months of hard work, disappointment and elation, worry and financial burden for her.

She is a member of the World Crafts Council and is a highly-skilled craftswoman, expert at spinning in wool and silk and in nearly all the crafts taught at the Centre. She comes from a family of craftsworkers, and learned her skills in the way they were taught for centuries — through the natural handing-down of knowledge from generation to generation.

Today this natural teaching process has been arrested by our way of life. The practice of traditional crafts no longer occupies a large part of people's leisure-time; it is dying out.

The situation had long troubled Mrs. Lovesey, but her ability to do something to help rectify it had been restricted over the past twenty-five years while she brought up her six children.

She gave lectures and demonstrations and over a year ago began teaching weaving, spinning and lace-making to children in a Bracknell school. But as she pointed out, this was not enough. So alone and without financial backing she set out to try and realise her long cherished dream.

In June 1968, when the idea of the Centre began to crystallise, Mrs. Lovesey was hoping, "that a group of interested people in and around the Reading area will contact me to discuss the setting up of a crafts centre. With their support and that of my family, bobbin and needle-point lace, weaving, spinning, tatting, traditional embroideries in all forms and crochet work could be taught."

Her aspirations were published in the Reading Mercury and Reading Chronicle newspapers and resulted in hundreds of letters from people offering support. She held a public meeting the following January and so many people turned up she had to hold a second one the same afternoon.

At last Mrs. Lovesey had sufficient offers of voluntary help from people expert in crafts to run classes. Her big problem was to find premises. Hours were spent in telephoning, and visiting different properties and people. There was no capital to draw upon except her own limited funds which were being rapidly drained away by expenses.

Then after months of worry her search was rewarded. Wokingham Town Council granted her a two-year lease on the former Civil Defence Headquarters in Denmark Street, as near ideal as she could have wished for.

The entrance is in the public car park and the back of the building overlooks a quiet garden. There are two large rooms where looms and work can be left undisturbed, plenty of storage space, a kitchen and an office.

Her family, friends and well-wishers helped to paint and prepare the Centre. A good deal of equipment was given or offered at cost price, and in April the Centre opened.

Today you may walk in at almost anytime of the day or evening and find an enthusiastic group of people industriously working at their crafts. It is, as Mrs. Lovesey envisaged, an informal club to be enjoyed by everyone, from eight to eighty.

Membership entitles people to any advice they require about their work, and to the use of the Centre as and when they wish during the days it is open — with the exception of the evening, when the noisy craft of lapiduary work (stone polishing) is carried out.

The annual membership fee is £2-10s. per person, with reduced rates for families, students and old age pensioners. Specialist tuition is 7s. 6d. for a one-and-a-half hour session.

The Centre is run by volunteers and is completely non-profit making. At present it has been turned into an Association as the first step towards being made a charity. This would make it eligible for a grant from the World Crafts Council. It is self-supporting, but with the number of members at present, it can only just keep 'in the black'.

Its members vary from eight-year-olds to an eighty-year-old granny, housewives to university students. Its visitors come both from this country and abroad, often as a result of the regular accounts of the Centre that appear in the World Crafts Council's international magazine.

The Centre is open from 10.30 to 5.30 on Thursdays and Fridays; on Wednesdays from 10.30 to 8.30 and on Tuesdays from 10.30 to 9.30. On Mondays it is closed.

FIG 6.15 This really tells its own story

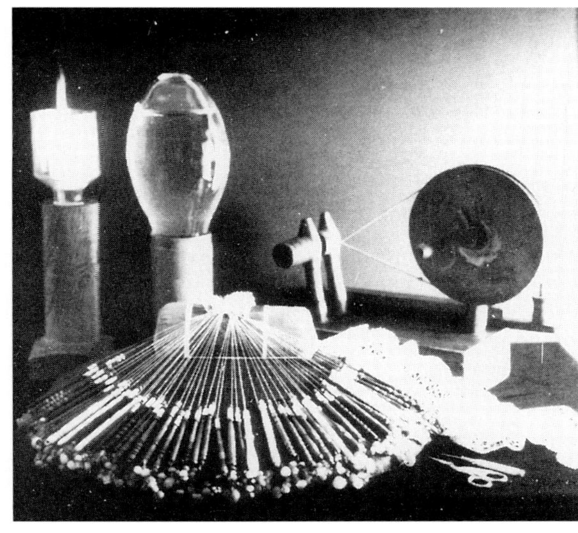

FIG 6.16 Close-up of pillow shown on page 37 with light, flask and winder

The Crafts Council of Great Britain Ltd

47 Victoria Street London SW1   01 799 1502

President: HRH The Duke of Edinburgh KG

Director: Cyril Wood OBE   6th June, 1969

Mrs. Lovesey,
Berkshire Craft Centre,
Denmark Street Car Park,
WOKINGHAM, Berkshire.

Dear Mrs. Lovesey,

I feel I must write at once to tell you how much
I was impressed by what you are doing at the
Craft Centre, and how stimulated I was by what I
saw there.   Few things have encouraged me more
than the complete absorption and concentration of
the four little girls of nine in lace-making.
The people of Wokingham and elsewhere in Berkshire
are indeed fortunate in having facilities for
craft work so easily and cheaply available, and
they owe it all to your vision and determination.
You are putting into practice what I have been
advocating for a long time, and what I have seen
you doing so splendidly with so little means
strengthens my own determination to establish
craft centres in other parts of the country.

I have written to the Town Clerk telling him of my
interest and admiration, and I have suggested my
coming to see him in the course of the next few weeks
to see what we can do together to ensure the future
of your Centre, and its further development. I
shall continue to think how the Crafts Council (with
similarly small means!) might be able to assist, and
I will get in touch with you again as soon as I have
something practical to suggest.

Meanwhile I send you my warmest congraulations and
best wishes for a happy and successful future.

Yours sincerely,

CYRIL WOOD (Director)

FIG 6.17 Letter from the Crafts
Council of Great Britain

FIG 6.18 Wedding veil made by the Author while at South Hill Park Art Centre, under the watchful eye of Cathy Barley, Doreen Holmes and Pat Gibson

Royal County of Berkshire

Department of Education

Kennet House 80-82 King's Road Reading RG1 3BL

Telephone Reading (0734) 55981

Your reference

My reference   AJWL/VC

When calling ask for   Mr Legge

4 March 1976

Dear Mrs Lovesey

Early in September the Department of Education and Science is
organising a course at Bulmershe College of Higher Education for
people in the education services of most of the countries in
Western Europe. One aspect of the course is work done by
"animateurs" who, in France, are often unpaid people, almost
always not directly connected with the official education services,
who go into a community and establish some worthwhile group such
as the Craft Centre in Wokingham. Your own efforts represent one of
the best examples of "animateurism" I know of, and I wonder if it
would be possible, if the D.E.S. wishes, for course members to visit
the Craft Centre, see it in operation, and chat to the members and
organisers.

One of the problems is the date — 12th–18th September — and the fact
that the visits would almost certainly have to be evening ones.

Three questions:

1. Would you be open at that time of the year?
2. Would you let course members visit the craft centre?
3. Would there be, in the evening, both members and
   organisers available?

Best wishes for your future success.

Yours sincerely

A J W Legge
Adult Education Adviser

Mrs N Lovesey
16 Woodrow Drive
WOKINGHAM

FIG 6.20 'Flowers of Gold'. Cathy Barley worked these pockets in gold thread, along with the tie belt and tassels, for her City and Guilds Textile Exam. in 1980

FIG 6.19 The answers to the questions asked in Mr Legge's letter were: (1) Yes, we were; (2) Yes, we would; (3) Always. About 25 animateurs from Western Europe came, the verdict was, a grand time was had by all

FIG 6.21 'Whoops'

FIG 6.22 Swan by Nina Devereux

FIG 6.23 Nina Devereux designed the clown to end my last book. This book being for my grand-daughters, what could be more appropriate than her design of Flower Fairies which she is working around the four corners of a tablecloth. Maybe one day it will be used by her grand-daughters

Once old and growing even older,
reflecting on the past
causes confusion with reality.
Reflections, more real now
than in that instant of happening,
and only age will prove the truth of this.
Youth is too busy growing old, to
consciously think about reflecting
on the little time they have had
to reflect on, but the camera you call your mind,
is clicking, developing and recording
from the instant you draw breath
until someone blows out the candle.

Appendix I

The following information was compiled by Hilary Rickets, of Larkfield Crafts, and she would like to share it with you.

It is not easy to make thread comparisons, as each type of thread has its own inherent qualities. These vary with each manufacturer and depend on the different types of processing they are subject to. For instance:

Mettler gives a soft finish
Molynleke gives a crisp firm finish
Brillante is somewhere between the two
Wigleys is very soft
Egyptian Gassed Cotton is very crisp
Sizes as different as 100 or 80 cordonnet *Fil a Dentelles*, Mettler 30, Tanne 30, Brillante 30, Molynleke 40, Linen 70, 80, 90, can all be used on the same size graph but the results will be vastly different. The higher or tighter the twist, the firmer the lace produced.

Thread measurement

Indirect system
The indirect system = length to weight
∴ 1 lb of thread = 50 miles of thread – called size 50
∴ 1 lb of thread = 1 mile of thread – called size 1

English Cotton System
840 yards = 1 hank
∴ The number of hanks to the 1 lb weight = the count
3 hanks to the 1 lb = size 3

Woollen Count
256 yards = 1 hank

Worsted Count
560 yards = 1 hank
∴ The number of hanks to the 1 lb weight = the count

Direct System
9000 metres = 1 gramme = 1 denier
9000 metres weighing 15 grames = 15 denier

Twists
S twist yarn = clockwise twist
Z twist yarn = anti-clockwise twist

S twist – S plyed = balanced thread
S twist – Z plyed = unbalanced thread, and this gives a crinkled yarn

Mercerised Cotton
Yarn passed through baths of caustic soda and the fibres open up. The number of times this is repeated depends on the depth of colour required. It is then put through hot rollers to polish.

Appendix II

DMC Cordonnet	DMC Perle	DMC Brillante	DMC Retors	DMC Fil a Dentelles	Filato di Canter	Madeira Tanne	Mettler	Molnlyeke	Sylko	Brok	Egyptian Gassed (Belgium)	Wigley	Bockens	Bone	Campbells	Barbour	Gütermann	Fine Silk	Madeira Rayon
	5									16/2									
10	8																		
20																			
30																			
40	12																		
50				30								35/2		40					
60												40/2	30	50					
70									24/3					60		40/3			
80			70/80									50/2		70					
100													50						
												60/2							
									36/3				60		100/3	100/3			
	30	30			30	30						80/2		100					
	30	30			30	30						80/2		100					
									36/2			90/2	80						
							40	40	60/2				100					40	
	50	50			50				100/3	60									
						60			80/2	70									
					80				100/2	80							210/2		
										90									
									120/2	100									
											120								
									140/2	120									
											140								
									160/2	140									
									180/2	160									
										170	180								

Suppliers

Alby Lace Centre
Cromer Road
Alby
Norwich
Norfolk

Frank Herring & Sons
27 High West Street
Dorchester
DT1 1UP

Honiton Lace Shop
44 High Street
Honiton
Devon

D J Hornsby
149 High Street
Burton Latimer
Kettering
Northants

Capt J R Howell
19 Summerwood Lane
Halsall
Nr Ormskirk
Lancs L39 8RG

Larkfield Crafts
4 Island Cottages
Mapledurwell
Basingstoke
RG25 2LU

Loricraft
4 Big Lane
Lambourn
Berks
RG16 7XQ

Sebalace
76 Main Street
Addingham
Ilkley
West Yorks
LS29 0PL

Mace and Nairn
89 Crane Street
Salisbury
Wilts

The Lace Guild
The Hollies
53 Audnam
Stourbridge
West Midlands

D H Shaw
47 Zamor Crescent
Thurscroft
Rotherham
South Yorks

John & Jennifer Ford
5 Squirrels Hollow
Boney Way
Walsall

Shireburn Lace
Finkle Court
Finkle
Sherburn in Elmet
North Yorks

Newham Lace Equipment
15 Marlow Close
Basingstoke
Hants

B Phillips
Pantglas
Cellan
Lampeter
Dyfed

T Brown
Woodside
Greenlands Lane
Prestwood
Great Missenden
Bucks

A Sells
49 Pedley Lane
Clifton
Shefford
Beds

C & D Springett
29 Hillmorton Road
Rugby
Warwicks CV22 5BE

Enid Taylor
Valley House Craft Studio
Ruston
Scarborough
North Yorks YO13 9QE

George White
Delaheys Cottage
Thistle Hill
Knaresborough
North Yorks

English Lace School
Honiton Court
Rockbeare
Nr Exeter
Devon

Further reading

Raie Clare *The Dryad Book of Bobbin Lace* Dryad Press, London
Bridget Cook *Practical Skills in Bobbin Lace* Batsford, London
Bridget Cook & Geraldine Scott *The Book of Bobbin Lace Stitches* Batsford, London
Gillian Dye *Beginning Bobbin Lace* Dryad Press, London
Brigita Fuhrmann *Bobbin Lace* Watson-Guptill Publications, New York
Robin Lewis *101 Torchon Patterns* Dryad Press, London
Nenia Lovesey *Introduction to Needlepoint Lace* Batsford, London
Nenia Lovesey *Creative Design in Needlepoint Lace* Batsford, London
Nenia Lovesey *The Technique of Needlepoint Lace* Batsford, London
Peggy Martin *Bobbin Lace: Step-by-Step Basic* P. Martin
Pamela Nottingham *Bobbin Lace Making* Batsford, London
Pamela Nottingham *Technique of Bobbin Lace* Batsford, London
Valerie Paton *Creative Lace Patterns* Dryad Press, London
Marion Powys *Lace and Lace Making* Charles T. Branford Co., Boston
Alexandra Stillwell *Drafting Torchon Lace Patterns* Batsford, London
Jean Withers *Mounting and Using Lace* Dryad Press, London

Index